9/7

A Good Living

A Good Living

HUGH BARRETT

Foreword by Ronald Blythe
Drawings by Naomi Shaw

Old Pond Publishing

Published by
Old Pond Publishing
104 Valley Road, Ipswich IP1 4PA, United Kingdom
www.oldpond.com

Cover photograph courtesy of the author
Cover design by Liz Whatling
Text edited by Julanne Arnold
Typesetting by Galleon Typesetting
Printed and bound in Great Britain by
Biddles Ltd, Guildford and King's Lynn

Foreword

HUGH BARRETT's second volume of autobiography – the first was the excellent *Early to Rise* – will make compelling reading for anyone who knew the East Anglian countryside during the mid-twentieth century, and be an eye-opener for those who did not. It is only through such memoirs as this that the actual strangeness of the old agriculture can be conveyed. Or rather the curious personalities of those engaged in it, for the economic and work patterns remained much as they had been for generations. But the farmers themselves, so candidly caught in a young man's gaze and remembered so truthfully, were not at all like the farmers most of us meet now, but another race altogether. Whatever it was which made them different, a stronger sense of social class, a quite vanished idea of money and of being 'master', Barrett does not attempt to explain. Instead he gives the reader a fascinating (and now and then chilling) account of his employers in Essex and Suffolk, careful not to make them rural eccentrics, but revealing their characters and habits as a youngster from a non-farming background would have observed them. The pleasure of Hugh Barrett's writing is that it retains the kind of freshness which the people and places he describes had when he first glimpsed them. It possesses a kind of immediacy.

One of the signs of a natural writer is the ability to store up facts and impressions, sayings and first glimpses.

A Good Living is far more the result of Hugh Barrett's being able to contain within himself, as it were, so much of what he saw and did and heard during a whole series of jobs during the late 1930s onwards, than a piecing together of old notebooks. Hence its strength. The rules and techniques of the old farming are not inserted like history lessons but woven into the narrative in such a way that they become no more than the commonplaces of toil at this time. To be capable of showing the ordinariness as well as the oddness of existence at a particular moment is a great gift. Students of both human nature and farming practice can learn a lot here.

Especially readable are the descriptions of the old farms themselves, then on the verge of tumbling from everything they had known for hundreds of years into mechanization. Their little army of often miserably treated labourers was shrinking, their post-World War Two government protection growing. *A Good Living* is all about agriculture transition as the writer himself lived it. It is remarkably authentic throughout and an illuminating read. Even those who lived in the countryside during this period will see this book as a record of what they have forgotten, as well as a witty account of their youthful selves. But Hugh Barrett avoids everything to do with today's cult of the recent past, knowing as he does that it is founded on an ignorance of all that he – and his employers – stood for. Such as eating and smoking and drinking as much as you like, which was usually a lot! Here were the last of the big consumers not to connect anything they devoured with disease.

Some of Hugh Barrett's best writing is on seeds and

animals, on harvesting and marketing. He combines earthiness with vision and offers an accurate story of what it was like to at first find a farming job, and then to find his own farm at a time when the agricultural developments of the late twentieth century were inconceivable. Though professional in every respect where the land is concerned, he is not, of course, what might be called a typical farmer, but a man led by those ideals which have revitalized English village life since the days of William Cobbett and John Clare. *A Good Living* is one of those books which tell us how far we have come and, given the roller-coaster nature of farming, how far back we may have to go.

RONALD BLYTHE   *May 2000*

For my daughters and sons,
their spouses and children,
and my great-grandchildren

and with thanks to Tim Shaw for all his help

Chapter One

Justices

JUSTICES HALL stood at the end of a narrow twisting lane in the middle of a small, close-cropped meadow with a shallow moat on one side and a row of old oak trees that hid the village church, on the other. When I first saw it, a Jersey cow and calf were grazing there and looked up as we drove by.

The house itself was separated from the meadow by iron park railings and an oval lawn with a drive running round it to the front door. In past times it would have been called a carriage sweep. Most of the house, and all the rear part, were sixteenth century: solid oak studs and beams, and patches here and there of pargeting. The front was different. At some point in the past, probably in the dying days of the nineteenth century, a fashion-conscious owner pushed out a large room either side of the front door with deep bay windows and a pillared porch. The general effect was one of modest affluence but slightly run-down; no fresh paint anywhere, and a bit dusty. A comfortable, generous sort of house. I write of it, of course, as I knew it sixty-odd years ago.

I was eighteen. My pupillage, served on Home Farm, an estate of one thousand acres of light land in East Suffolk, had ended and I was now manager-designate of

1

Justices Hall, land and livestock, in the county of Essex.

It was 1935. Farming was in a bad way and with unemployment high everywhere I was very lucky to find anyone willing to give me a job of any kind. On leaving Home Farm I put an advertisement in the *Farmer and Stockbreeder* and the same day the magazine came out, the manager of Justices drove over to Hertfordshire, interviewed me and then drove me to north-east Essex and a job for which my qualifications were minimal. I soon found that the difference between being pupil to a hard-up working farmer and managing for a 'gentleman farmer' was considerable.

The first shock came as we drove up to the house. A short pudgy man in a worn grey suit with a collar and black tie, flat cap and a pipe clenched between his teeth was pushing a lawn mower on the oval lawn. I remarked to my companion, Peter the departing manager, that I was glad there was a gardener, but was swiftly told that it was the Boss, Euan Lentner. I reeled slightly. A farmer mowing a garden lawn? None I knew would dream of being seen in a garden, let alone sweating in it. My ideas would need adjusting.

After putting my bags in my room and getting washed and brushed, I went downstairs to the dining room for lunch. The room had been the old court room which gave Justices its name. Large, square, with windows overlooking the farmyard and a wood fire burning in a cavernous chimney. To judge by the many holes in the thick red Turkey carpet, the fire had been throwing sparks for a generation. On the walls were sporting prints depicting top-hatted gentry mounted on improbable horses leaping over impossible hedges: 'Full cry', 'Up and Over', 'In at the Kill'. At one end of

2

the room a highly polished mahogany sideboard was decorated with silver trophies – Champions and Supreme Champion Essex Saddleback pigs, won at county and national shows. There was also a massive Stilton cheese and an empty tantalus.

The Boss was looking out of the window as I came in and didn't turn until Peter said, 'Euan, this is Hugh Barrett.' At this, he moved, shook hands and muttered 'Howdydo' as he sat down. He enquired whether the journey had been all right, remarked the weather was improving, asked for the salt and that was the sum total of the table conversation. Not, I thought, a very lively start.

I had not been told what the living was like, but as soup was followed by roast saddle of mutton, and in turn apple pie and cream, a nibble of cheddar and biscuits, then coffee, I realized it was excellent indeed. A pretty cap and aproned serving maid, with another and a cook in the back of beyond, was vastly different from Home Farm. Mr Lentner kept a good table; I was happy indeed to have my feet under it. Lunch over and having smoked the cigarettes which the Boss offered, Peter and I went out to look at the farm.

It was in the order of three hundred acres. I never did know the exact acreage because the farm existed for pig breeding and this took up only a small proportion of the land and that was on the light gravelly soil nearest to the farm buildings and house. As we walked through them, Peter explained that the sows were out the year round but spent the last month of pregnancy each in a separate paddock with a wooden ark for shelter when they farrowed. Euan believed in breeding healthy, hardy stock and this spartan system achieved it. The snag was

3

that the paddocks had become infested with intestinal worms. There were twenty paddocks, ten on each side of a cart track with a meal shed and concrete water reservoir in the middle.

Gilts farrowed in buildings round the yard where an eye could be kept on them. When a litter was due it was routine to look at the gilt last thing at night. This was among the things I only learned in time – a short time though, because Peter was leaving for South Africa within ten days.

'What's the Boss really like?'

'He's all right . . . no he's more than all right. He's a jolly decent chap. You'll never know him though. I've been here three years and I don't, but it doesn't seem to matter. He lets you get on with the job. You'll be okay.'

4

This was reassuring because I didn't know what to make of the man of so few words.

In all there were about eighty breeding females. They were running in two meadows, the best with an Essex Saddleback boar, and those not up to the pedigree standard with a Large White boar called Norfolk.

Sows and gilts were all pedigree Essex which, in my quickly acquired opinion, were infinitely superior to their rivals the Wessex Saddlebacks, which have no white socks on their hind legs and no white tip to their tails. Wessex ears tended to be longer than the Essex and their white saddles were, in the opinion of breeders, less well defined and not so neat. Incidentally, gilts – which I once heard a lady explain to her teenage daughter were 'Girl pigs not old enough to be married' – were called yelts, a pronunciation I've not met elsewhere.

The pigs were on light gravelly soil and the rest of the farm was heavy London clay. Dig down and it came up blue. Years ago the land, now all down to grass, had been ploughed on the eight-furrow stetch and this still showed as broad-topped rolling waves, the 'valleys' providing the drainage. Peter showed me a few rather inferior grazing cattle. It was obvious cattle had no great part in the economy of the farm.

There were two woods – Ash Plant and Bog Wood, which with the rough pastures harboured game and rabbits. Ash Plant was growing only ash pole with an undergrowth of hazel. It was regularly coppiced, the poles sawn into four-foot lengths for the dining room fire, the trash burned on the spot and the hazel given to an old thatcher, Willy Cracknel, to make what he called springels. I used the Suffolk word broaches, pronounced

5

brorchers. Willy could split a hazel wand and twist it into a U-shape at an incredible speed. He reckoned to do a thousand a day.

At the wet end of Bog Wood a spring was the source of a stream which ran alongside and then down to a field below the house where a hydraulic ram was set to pump water up to the house and to the paddocks' reservoir. Rams are wonderful things relying on the energy in a large volume or head of water to pump up smaller amounts. Since they work night and day and go on for years without attention they are a very cheap form of power indeed. I found the steady 'thunk, thunk, thunk', a sound just audible from my bedroom window on a still night, strangely reassuring.

Peter told me about the men. It didn't take long. 'We've only got two, Pinnock and Shinn. Pinnock is the old fellow who is probably mixing grub ready for tomorrow. He is good. Very steady, well . . . slow but absolutely reliable. He can do everything bar castrating and worming.' 'Yes . . . but who does the castrating,' I asked. 'You do!' I was taken aback. 'For God's sake man, I've never castrated a thing in my life.' And might have added that I had no eager desire to do so. Peter said, 'Don't fret, there's a bunch to do tomorrow. I'll soon show you. It's not difficult once you know how and so long as your knife is sharp.

'Shinn, the other man, does a bit of everything: carts the straw, mucks out and looks after the paddock and meadow fences. And he milks the house cow, separates the cream and cleans the boots, yes, and he does the kitchen garden.' Having been used to a labour force of just on fifty and working regularly with a dozen, I wondered how I should get on with just two men. And I wondered how they would get on with a raw youth like me.

That was about all I got from Peter that day. It was five o'clock and we went indoors to the sitting room where the Boss was drinking a long whisky and soda.

'There's sherry or gin if you'd rather. Peter drinks sherry. Help yourselves.' I had never before been invited to make such a choice and help myself. I rather liked it. It was Euan's custom to drink whisky at tea time – there was never any tea – and just before dinner he had a Martini with a cherry on a stick.

The room had the same rather dingy cream-coloured walls with more sporting prints, 'Gone Away', 'Gone to Earth' and 'Ware Wire'. Since Euan had not the slightest interest in hunting or any other sports this choice of pictures was strange. The only non-sporting one was a portrait in oils of a heavy jowled and pompous old buffer – Euan's father – who looked eminently at home in his heavy embossed and gilded frame. He had been a liveryman and 'something substantial' in the City.

Sipping my drink I noted the bookshelves with the *Cyclopaedia of Modern Agriculture* (twelve volumes), Youatt on *The Pig*, Primrose McConnel's *Handbook of Agriculture*, John Evelyn's *Silva – a Discourse on Forest Trees* and Wrightson's *Sheep Management*, all of which I remember well because Euan gave them to me when I left: I have them yet. In the middle of one shelf a copy of Marie Stopes's *Married Love* caught my eye. Surely an odd volume to find in such a bachelor establishment?

On a table in the window embrasure copies of the farming papers plus *Punch*, *Country Life* and *Esquire* – a somewhat salacious periodical and, like *Married Love*, not usually found displayed in respectable farm house-holds. It was a comfortable room. Heavy leather club armchairs which like the red Turkey carpet had suffered puppies and boots. A vaguely Adam fireplace and beside it a well-stocked drinks cupboard. I stood glass in hand for a long time taking it all in and looking out of the window over the lower part of the farm across meadows and woods and away into the distance where the sky reflected light from the invisible estuary of the Blackwater. Five mallard flew overhead.

The sound of a gong brought us to the dining room again. I felt the formality which spotless linen tablecloth and napkins, heavy silver and three wine glasses induces, a bit overpowering. It was all so vastly different from the domestic regime at Home Farm that in a way I almost resented it. We sat down. The food was delicious. My first experience of scallops. There was a fowl with roast potatoes and spinach and a splendid ginger suet pudding with lemon sauce.

The dishes were brought in by Betty, a curly haired girl of sixteen. Peter said thank you; Euan said nothing. Betty's sister, the other maid, was eighteen, her name, Mona. Euan called her Lisa. But he never addressed either of them if he could help it. Nor did the cook get the benefit of direct communication. Euan spoke of her as Mrs Whatsername, and I've now forgotten what her real name was. The fact is, Euan didn't like women and wanted as little as possible to do with them. In this he was remarkably successful.

After dinner he raised the question of wages. Rather diffidently as if it were a subject he didn't like discussing. 'Would a pound be all right?' 'Yes . . . of course, but didn't Peter tell you I know very little about pigs?'

(My wage at Home Farm had been five bob and I was embarrassed at the thought of getting paid so much when I was bringing so little to the job.)

Euan gave a sly sort of grin. 'Neither did he when he first came. Anyway, he can pass on what he knows to you in the ten days left before he sails . . . but it won't take that long! That reminds me, Peter. Get your photograph taken for the rogues gallery!' This was a row of four young men, previous managers, whose photographs stood on a side table. 'One other thing. You will be responsible for keeping the household accounts and paying the wages.' Peter interjected, 'Yes, and God help you ha! ha!'

A pound a week was a fortune. Hitherto I had managed to clothe myself and buy all the tobacco I wanted on five bob a week, so a pound was wealth, and add to that the unrestricted use of a car and all the food, wonderful food!

I went upstairs to a hot bath and bed thinking how undeservedly fortunate I was to find myself in such luxury. At Home Farm there was a bathroom off the dairy and I think I must have got into it three or four times in my year there. A cold, damp concrete floor and no water on tap. No wonder Justices looked uncommonly like paradise.

I soon got used to the small scale of the farming activities and could see that two men were enough to keep the place in what passed for reasonable condition. There was no urgency to make money, but that did not mean the Essex herd was a plaything.

Pinnock the herdsman was the most lugubrious man I'd ever met. He was over sixty, tall, gaunt and grey; everything about him was grey, dusted with pig meal.

A ragged grey moustache and a constant drip at the end of his nose completed the picture. But he was good at his job. If keeping records for the herdbook was beyond him, and he refused to do any castrating, he made up for it by knowing every mature pig on the place by sight and instinctively how to get the animals to do what he wanted and go where he required. He had a dog which shadowed him everywhere. It too was a greyish colour and looked vaguely unhappy and dispirited as if it had missed something in life. Pinnock used to eat his sandwiches sitting on an upturned bushel skip in the barn doorway, throwing the crusts to the dog who snatched them out of the air. So far as the day to day running of the herd went, I learned more from Pinnock than from Euan or Peter.

Shinn was a very different sort of man, a stocky chap always in collar and tie, his dungarees clean and his boots polished. He carried the clean-shaven air of one knowing himself to be superior, always 'correct', always right. He was the sort of man fitted for head gardener or chauffeur to a larger and more important establishment than Justices. I had very little to do with him. Satisfied with his own company, he rarely spoke unless it was necessary, even with Pinnock when they were working side by side.

There was a lot to learn and I had a lot of prejudice to be rid of. I had accepted what the Guv'nor at Home Farm thought of 'gentlemen farmers' – a pejorative term. They might be gentlemen but were rarely farmers. They existed to be robbed by their employees and, when opportunity offered, to be taken advantage of in deals with honest working farmers. It was a view so widely held as to be gospel.

There was too the world of difference between commercial pig farmers, who might merely be said to *keep* pigs, and pedigree pig breeders. The latter were likely to have private means, in itself a part qualification as 'gentlemen' regardless of how well or ill they farmed. Not all were dilettantes. Among them were men who took breeding seriously. They studied herd books, visited each other's herds and competed in local, county and national shows and prize rings.

The history of British agriculture is thick with names of gentlemen farmers who put their money and minds into livestock improvement. First the aristocracy encouraged competition among neighbours and tenants, and then later the lesser gentry and solid practical yeomen added their expertise and influence to create an awareness that good breeding mattered.

In his book *The Pig*, William Youatt puts it nicely: 'There is no question that for the improvement of livestock we were originally indebted to our hereditary landed aristocracy, The Earl of Carlisle and Lord Wenlock in Yorkshire, Lord Western in Essex, Lord Barrington in Berkshire and peers and squires prepared the way for rent-paying farmers.' But, he adds, 'At the present day the character of each breed is generally maintained on farms where pleasure and prize winning glory are combined with profit.'

In a footnote to the second edition of Youatt's book, his editor goes on to say: 'English agriculture owes much to the cold shades of opposition under which such men as Francis, Duke of Bedford, Coke of Holkham, Lord Yarborough, being excluded from favours of the Court and dignities of high office, found consolation in reclaiming wastes, breeding a bold tenantry,

11

and establishing an aristocracy of livestock.'

That was written in 1860 and although by 1935 the aristocracy had mostly forsaken the pig pens (although not the cattle ring), there were still plenty of gentlemen and yeoman farmers carrying on the good work of breed improvement.

We cut the boar piglets at eight weeks which was standard at the time. Nowadays most pigs whether for pork or bacon are left 'entire' but a sensitive palate will discern a certain rankness in the flavour and will choose meat from females. (The same is true of beef, as meat from heifers is superior to that from bulls.)

I quickly became a swift castrater, as the faster, the less pain. This operation and worming were the only times where Shinn, Pinnock and I all worked together. Shinn caught the pigs, and Pinnock held them up by the back legs and gripped them between his own while I did the cutting. The same thing for worming except that in this case the piglet was held head up while I administered a stinking drench of oil of chenopodium by means of a horn thrust down the throat. Very unpleasant gurgling sounds as they gagged and bubbled. They ought to have choked but never did. Both operations were accompanied by loud screams. Pain there must have been, but on release the pigs ran to the trough to feed. The memory of hurt inflicted was short.

We had few health problems except for erysipelas in the hot summer, but it never became serious. The medicine cupboard had a bottle of arsenic to be administered with care to put a fine gloss on the coats of show entries. There was also a bottle of strychnine but what that was intended for I don't know.

Pinnock's daily routine started with a quick look at

the newly farrowed pigs, then at the down farrowing ones and lastly at the fattening pens. Only the females producing reasonable size litters – a minimum of eight – and with good conformation and markings were kept in the herd register, and unless their female progeny came up to the mark, they were not bred from. The remaining females, poorly marked or perhaps lacking the required twelve dills (nipples), were fattened along with the males, or put to a Large White boar, whose blue and white progeny were fattened to around one hundred pounds and sold as porkers to local butchers.

I usually went round with Pinnock, but if I didn't he'd tell me of anything out of the way after breakfast. 'Sow in number 9 laid on two. Clumsy old davil: her mother done jest a same' or perhaps 'Us'll hatta knock the runt in number four on the hid. That 'on't do no good and she [the dam] ha' got enough to feed without him.'

The rest of the day he'd spend mixing meal, mucking out, cleaning pens and littering down the indoor pens with fresh wheat straw. If necessary he put straw in the outdoor paddocks. One of the most entertaining things to watch is down farrowing sows making up their beds. Serious and purposeful, they gather great jawfuls of straw and carefully arrange them in a nest. Some sows refuse to farrow in their huts, preferring, for what reason I cannot think, to produce their infants outside. I have seen a newly born litter suckling happily while snow fell thick on their dam's side. I tried to put them under cover but she was having none of it. We drove her into the ark, but as soon as we left the paddock she was out again with her fare. They all survived and flourished.

Chapter Two

Everyday Life

SINCE at first the Boss was silent and the men rarely spoke, it ought to have been dull. But after a while he relaxed and we talked a great deal after work in the evenings. He was a natural teacher with a lot of experience. I was happy to absorb all I could from him, not just about pigs but business, politics and all manner of worldly matters. He had no religious beliefs but professed himself happy that the churchyard was only the far side of the moat and wouldn't make too hard work for his coffin bearers. He was very positive that Communism was the most logical form of government and for that very reason it couldn't possibly work: an advanced view for the times.

Despite his misogamy he passed on some excellent advice about relationships with young women. 'Never think of marrying a girl until you've seen her mother' was one I took particular note of. He believed temperament passed through the female side of a union – true for pigs anyway. Another dictum, reinforced I'm sure by having had a series of youthful managers, went like this: 'Even if I wished to I couldn't stop you from what you want to do, but for Gawd's sake don't do it too near home!' Even if he had never suffered, he recognized the temptations.

Messages to cook or maids were passed through me. 'Tell Mrs Whatsername it's time she gave us a steak and kidney pudding.' Or, 'It's about time we had the partridges. They'll be too ripe if left much longer.' Mrs Whatsername continued to produce wonderful meals. Her raised pork pies decorated with pastry oak leaves and acorns were crisp and shining. Puddings of every sort included tarts and pies served with thick Jersey cream. As for drink, I will come to that later.

We ate a fair bit of game in season. Pheasant and partridge were hung in pairs in the netted game larder outside the kitchen north door until they acquired the desired degree of high flavour. In very cold weather they might be there for two weeks or more, in warmer times only a few days. In some extravagant households birds were hung by the neck in pairs, cock and hen together, and when one got so rotten it fell from the hook, that one was too ripe for eating and discarded, but the other one just right. Personally I'll take mine before it can be smelled from the far side of the yard. On this Euan and I agreed.

Euan had firm opinions about food, often repeating his dictum, 'Pig once a day, and potatoes twice.' There was always bacon for breakfast but in addition a large ham on the sideboard, and it was a slice or two of this, pink with at least a half-inch of white fat, with which he finished his meal.

I ought, perhaps, to have felt guilty at living so well at a time when so many were going hungry. That it did not make me think harder about economics and justice must be put down to my being young and unaware.

There was more than enough evidence of how bad things were. Imported grain was coming into the country at prices lower than the cost of growing it here. The Russians, I was told, delivered barley for even less than the cost of threshing our own. They wanted our sterling to buy our machinery, and they starved millions of their people in doing so.

Our only regular outing was to one of Euan's cousins for Sunday dinner, for which I struggled into a dinner jacket and dickey left behind by a former manager. Here I saw how the seriously rich lived and felt slightly prejudiced against them until I heard that the cousin had bought four Austin Sevens for the exclusive use of the domestic staff. His argument was that no one could be expected to stay working in a place so far from any town unless they could get away from time to time. Very enlightened, I thought, and nice to have money in such abundance it could be spent in that way.

In good weather we often walked round the pens and paddocks after dinner. This was when I really learned what an Essex should look like. After a few weeks Euan began to test me. We'd go to a pen where a dozen or so gilts were being got ready for a breed show or perhaps the Essex or Suffolk Show. 'Now which of those would you choose to enter?' And I'd try point by point to select the three I thought best.

Modestly, I became quite good at weighing up the relative good and bad points: 'Ears too pricked (or too floppy). Rather short in the back. Saddle too narrow.' Euan would give his opinion and add a word of encouragement. He thought I had an eye for the job and I was rather proud of that. He was an official judge and had a name for professional impartiality. Some judges were suspected of allowing commercial consid-erations to influence their award of rosettes; the well-known and long-established 'You scratch my back and I'll scratch yours.'

Getting animals ready for shows or the sale ring was an art. Pinnock cleaned them, oiled their coats – already shiny with arsenic! – and should a white blemish appear where all should be black, I suspect he used a touch of boot polish. Not done of course . . . but it was; perhaps not many were taken in by such a mild and common trick.

The other half of preparing pigs for the show ring is to train them for it. Pinnock spent hours doing it. Picture a ring with three or more herdsmen, each with a pig, trying to keep his animal moving round as much as possible in front of the judge. That was difficult enough, but some classes required two or even three pigs from each competitor in the ring at the same time, pigs all more interested in each other than in what the herdsman wanted them to do. Sometimes it was chaotic and judges were wont to use harsh language to men who failed to control their charges. Pinnock was good in the show ring although his habitually mournful expression never changed even when a First, or better, a Champion rosette was awarded.

Euan's herd had the prefix 'Justice' and was primarily known for breeding females. It is a mystery how it was that since all breeders had of necessity to produce males and females, some were consistently more successful with one sex than the other. We had one boar bred on the farm, Justice Dictator 2nd, but he was used only on bought-in females. There were two other boars, one bred in Yorkshire and the other in south Essex, and it required nice judgement to know which of them should be used on any given female. Conformation was all important. Twelve tits on the boar are just as important as on the female. The markings and the way ears and tail are carried, ham depth and length of back are also part of the equation.

Dictator – a reflection of the times? – cropped up in many herds, but more noble-sounding names were commoner. There were Duchesses and Grand Duchesses, Emperors, Dukes, Lady this and Lady that, paying tribute as it were to the earlier aristocratic breeders. At one time Justices had all those grand female names, but also the plebeian Rose, Emily, Lavender and many more.

Within a few years the custom of giving classy names to pigs had almost vanished. No more Grand Dukes, Countesses, even the equally evocative Lilac or Lavender ceased to be heard. Today, if a pig is to be identified at all, it is by a stainless steel numbered ear clip – and where's the romance in that?

Justice Lavender 1st was memorable. She left a strong, long line behind her. I've seen a breeder point to a gilt or sow and say 'She's got a touch of Justice Lavender in her, wouldn't you think?' A glance at the catalogue where the pedigree was outlined would reveal all, but it earned respect if you could tell something of the blood line just by looking. I think Lavender's mark was in rather specially neat ears.

As time went by I was accepted and my status confirmed as belonging in the judging ring as a sort of probationer. These were lovely times. The grunt and squeal of pigs, the genial banter of breeders, a lot of 'Well young man, you've got a pretty pen of gilts there; nicely got up too. Decent herdsman, old Pinnock.' It was the done thing to congratulate the herdsman as well as the breeder. Rightly so: presentation counted.

18

I was at Smithfield the year when the Champion – or it may have been the Supreme Champion – Aberdeen Angus was found to have injections of wax under the skin of its back making it smooth with no disfiguring hollows. A herdsman had blabbed and the scandal had been exposed. Drink had something to do with it. Herdsmen were usually given a show allowance and a fair bit commonly went on drink. They needed it too. Sleeping on straw by their charges for perhaps a week wasn't all fun. The Wax Affair was talked of for years.

All farms had rats and most have today although warfarin – a poison invented for use against human enemies in the Second World War – now makes control pretty efficient. Justices had rats and where they were thickest and get-at-able we gassed them with cymag. This was chiefly under the paddock water tank and meal shed. They made a ghastly wheezing sound as the gas took effect: not a pleasant death I'd say.

One sharp morning, Shinn being off sick, I went out to milk the Jersey house-cow, a quiet beast housed in a loose box to one side of the yard. Leaving by the back door I noticed a rat run along the low garden wall and I thought, casually, that rats weren't often seen there. As I opened the loose box door there was a scurry of feet and two rats shot across the floor to hide behind the feed bin. Another ran up the wall and onto the rafters. Several more tried to get past me and out into the yard; one went under the door. It would not have been unusual to see one or two rats in that box, but half a score was unprecedented. And what struck me was that these rats *didn't know their way round*. They were not skipping along the normal well-trodden routes, but were plainly confused. They were strangers: aliens.

I got on with the milking but with my head pressed into the cow's flank rats appeared and disappeared across my field of vision. I was finishing stripping the last drops into the pail when Pinnock stuck his head round the door. 'Th'ole dawg ha' killed hell know how many rats. They're everywhere. Buggers even in th'oil shed. I dussent hardly go into the barn. We'll hatta do suthin quick!'

I carried the milk indoors and returned to have a look. Pinnock had not exaggerated. Truly the rats were everywhere: we were infested. You couldn't move sack or bag, empty or full, without at least one rat jumping out in search of safety. By eight o'clock Pinnock and I and his dog had killed scores, but it was terribly clear that for every one we slaughtered there were ten more left.

More drastic measures would have to be taken so I sent word to the village that anyone with a good ratter – or even without – would be welcome to join the fray. I told Euan what was afoot but he declined to assist, saying he was frightened of rats. (So was I, and so I am even now.)

For the rest of the day six men, a horde of kids and heaven knows how many dogs killed and killed, first round the buildings, barn, yards and pens and then up in the paddocks. How many? Hundreds for sure, perhaps a thousand. (They were gathered in heaps but no one was keen to count them.) By next morning the great mass had gone. There was the odd 'stranger' and the normal 'locals' but the rest had vanished.

What we had witnessed was one of those rare mass rat migrations which sometimes get reported in local papers. They always happen at night but where they

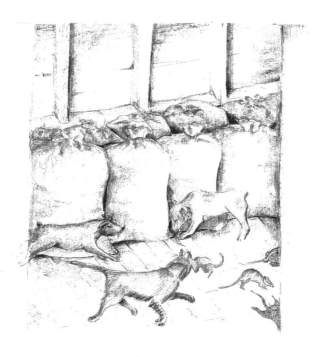

come from and why they migrate en masse and then disperse to vanish as they commonly do, nobody seems to know.

'Pigs can smell the wind' is an old and true saying. It was the scent from a young gilt on heat in the pens in a distant yard which caught the questioning snout of Norfolk, the Large White boar, a perfume impossible to ignore. It was at night when I was woken by Mona knocking on my door. She was trembling. 'There's a horrible noise in the yard, we don't know what it is and we're frightened!' I got up, stuck my head out of the window and true enough a frightful racket was going on. Mona, looking very pretty and demure in her white cotton nightdress (I remember it perfectly), whisked past the door as I pulled on my breeches and set off downstairs to investigate.

Halfway up the yard by the fitful light of the moon I could see the cause of the ruction. Norfolk, in his eagerness to get to the oestrous gilt, had tried to lift the five-bar meadow gate from its hinges and in doing so had got his head and one front leg trapped through the bars. Unable to back out of his dilemma, he simply carried it with him out of the meadow, up the cart track and into the yard where he was finally baulked by the iron gate standing between him and his desire.

My concern was to free him from the gate before he damaged himself more than he already might have. It was useless to attempt pushing or pulling. Eight foot long, he weighed at least four hundred pounds and wasn't cooperating anyway. In the end I fetched a saw, cut through the bars and he got free. Did he then head back to his meadow? Not at all. He had a fixed idea of where his duty lay and it took a few good jabs with a pitch fork before I got him into a pen. The five-bar oak gate must have weighed a hundredweight, but the strength of a boar the size of Norfolk would easily carry it. I've seen him flip a heavy cast-iron trough with his snout, tossing it six foot at a time.

Pigs are not stupid – except that they trust their keepers. The 'Educated Pig' was a common attraction at fairs and circuses, and early in the 1800s two unusual acts earned a lot of attention. An eccentric farmer trained four hogs to draw a small chaise-cart from his home to the Woolsack in St Albans, where they were rewarded with a trough of beans and mash. After two hours of rest and refreshment for owner and animals, the hogs were re-harnessed and driven round the town to the astonishment and admiration of the crowd. The farmer indignantly refused an offer of fifty pounds for the team, which was a lot of money at that time.

The other clever pig demonstrated a keen sense of smell. Sir Henry Mildmay's gamekeeper trained a sow to 'point' at game. She was much more accurate at detecting game than dogs bred for the purpose and would stand to pheasants and partridges, snipe and rabbits but never to hare. Quite frequently Slut – for that was her name – would point game the dogs had missed. She was a black sow and lived to attain a weight of seven hundred pounds, finally dispatched when suspected of having killed and eaten some newborn lambs.

I had financial problems – with the household accounts. It was established practice to sit down with Mrs Whatsername on the first Monday of the month to sort out the bits of paper – receipts for boot polish, silver polish, brass polish, wax polish, flour, suet, sugar, bacon, beef, mutton etc. – having not the slightest idea

whether the sums on paper approximated to the real costs. My concern was to arrive at a point where expenditures balanced with what was left in the float.

The first two months' accounts balanced nicely and I was shocked when Euan said I'd cooked them! 'Don't get hot under the collar. I'm only suggesting from long experience here that the accounts have never balanced without jiggering with the figures.' He added kindly, 'I don't suppose I could do any better myself, but it's good exercise for you and keeps Mrs Whatsername on her toes.'

The hard part for me was listening to that good lady explaining every month just why we got through so much boot polish. 'It's Shinn,' she'd say. 'He lards it on without thinking what it costs, and you just see how his boots is new polished – every morning.' Shinn was out of favour in the kitchen and I don't think I was thought a lot of either. That's not surprising for Mrs Whatsername was three times my age and had seen several of my predecessors tangled in the accounts.

Euan left me to buy the pig feed but guided me in the way I should go about it. Merchants large and small put so many reps on the road that it wasn't out of the ordinary for four or five to call on a single day. With the breeding herd and all the fattening pigs, Justices' order was worth having. I might have bought it all from one firm but Euan insisted it should be spread about among several. So instead of single orders of tons of barley meal, middlings, flaked maize or bean meal and so on, the order was broken down into half ton lots and even smaller parcels in the case of more concentrated feed such as fishmeal.

Euan said, 'It won't make any of them fat but a little is better than nothing. It gives the poor devils something to show their bosses they've been trying.' I found ordering such small amounts – or none at all – embarrassing: in fact I hated it. Euan admitted he did too, which is why he passed the job to me. 'I don't keep a dog and bark too,' he used to say. The majority of the reps knew little about what they were selling. They were cheap untrained labour and would probably have been as happy or miserable selling brushes.

I enjoyed mixing the pig food, tipping bags of barley meal, middlings, bean meal, flaked maize and fishmeal or Vitamealo – a popular concentrate – into a big conical heap and then with Pinnock turning it to make a rich homogeneous whole. Outside the mixing shed were very large wooden tubs, each holding about sixty gallons. The meal was added to water in them and stirred to a nice porridge. This semi-liquid we then carried in buckets and poured into the troughs. (The relative amounts of each ingredient and the amount fed depended on whether it was for breeding or fattening stock.) Carrying heavy, wet-handled buckets in bitter March winds was no cure for chilblains. In the summer if any wet meal got left in the bottom of the tub for a day or two, a swarm of very unpleasant white maggoty creatures appeared in it. They were associated with a distinctive sour smell. I'm reminded of it when offered bourbon; good stuff gone off!

Once the demands made by the herd were satisfied, Euan allowed me to use time left over for whatever I wanted to do. Of course pigs did take up most of every day but whenever possible I slipped away to the woods – especially Bog Wood. Bog Wood was ten acres and as the name suggests a damp place. There was a spring at the far end, the source of the stream which fed the hydraulic ram and ran alongside the meadows where dry sows and the boars lived.

At some time in the distant past, a small area of the wood just inside the wicket gate had been laid out as a pleasaunce. There was a shed rather like a summer-house overlooking a bank of rhododendrons and azaleas and beyond this a winding path leading to a straight eighteen foot wide ride which ran the entire length of the wood. Euan with hook and scythe kept it clear – one of the few labouring jobs he ever did. There were old elms and oaks, a few hollies and a scatter of old ash and 'pole' ash – that is, growth from the stools of previously felled ash trees.

My favourite spot was halfway down the drive within the arms of an ancient elm felled a long time ago by winter gales. Ivy grew from the high branches and trailed down to make a curtain: a private room from which I could see without being seen, for within it was deeply shaded. I sat many times under that ivy-clad tent and watched an old hare come 'himping' down the ride towards me taking side bites at young ash plants as he came, and quite oblivious of me until suddenly his ear would go up and he froze, until suspicion confirmed, his ears down, he dashed for the safety of the undergrowth.

Hares are strange creatures. In winter they move hump backed, sadly and slowly along the hedgerows and ditch banks, but in springtime, no longer solitary, they gather in jocund groups of a score and more and play tag, chasing each other round and round. Standing tall on hind legs they box with their front paws until, tiring of running and fisticuffs, they break off to feed until the urge for furious activity returns. They go on like this for hours.

At these times the March Hare acts mad and is less timid than usual. There is something secret and unknowable about them and perhaps for this reason in ancient times they had a bad reputation. In Britain, witches could turn into hares as easily as they did cats. One American witch gave birth to a hare and English ones were accused of the same sin, for which they were duly hanged or burned.

I like hares. They are magic and unless they are damaging a crop or there is a call from the kitchen for jugged hare, I will not shoot them. They are not a popular meat among country people – at least not in East Anglia, where they are commonest: 'Too bloody', they say. Germans consume huge numbers.

Keeping quiet behind my green ivy curtain I watched tree creepers working the rough bark of elms and oaks and green woodpeckers – the yaffle – hammering and drumming dead trees in search of insect grubs or making a nesting hole. I was happy just sitting there, watching birds flit from tree to tree, swooping and gliding in the aerial chambers under the canopy of tall trees. That was summer. In heavy winter winds I often chose to stand close to a grand old oak. The boughs shook and moved, creaking and complaining as the gale roared overhead. I imagined I could feel its roots struggling to hold the massive superstructure firm.

Every day, winter and summer, I walked from the yard to the Bog Wood main drive and then halfway down turned left towards the meadow with the boar and sows. The path stopped at a stile on the edge of the wood immediately in front of the stream. From there I could see and count all the pigs without walking further. There was a rail-fence on the far side of the stream where pheasants and partridges perched companiably together, fluffing out their dew-wet feathers to dry in the sun. The cock pheasants' breasts glowed bronze and their blue and green neck feathers and scarlet wattles flashed as they preened. At that place I once watched a mole swim across the stream, its digging paws going like short paddles. This was one of those moments in early summer when the dawn chorus was finished and for a while the fields and woods were silent.

Woodcock favour dark damp places and were common in Bog Wood. Euan liked both woodcock and snipe and would ask me to bag one or two. He was a poor shot and the woodcocks' erratic flight was beyond him. The same with snipe which haunted the unkempt low meadows. They rose swiftly from the wet grass and rushes to take off in a rapid zig-zag flight, dodging, twisting and turning and hard to hit. Euan could never come near them.

Snipe and woodcock were not to my liking. The traditional method is to cook them whole, plucked but not drawn, innards (the 'trail') and all, and eat them on toast. Actually, to describe the process as cooking is to exaggerate. Euan said 'Tell Mrs Whatsername not to overdo them: just show them the fire and have the toast hot and ready!' Not for me. How can one know a thing tastes of worms without ever having eaten one? I was certain I could and found it unpleasant.

Whenever Euan was at home – he had business interests in London as well as the farm – he would join me and walk round the whole herd, often for no better reason than the pleasure it gave. Good stockmen all do this. It looks like idle ambling, but all the time information is being gathered and observations made and subconsciously stored away for when use might be made of them.

Our walk followed a pattern. First to the paddocks and the down farrowing sows, or sows and their new litters rooting in the grass or asleep in the arks. Then to the indoor pens. Second litters were usually born in the paddocks but we liked gilts to have their first fare indoors. Not so much for the sake of warmth but to be handy to the house and quickly reached if there was trouble. An inexperienced female may flop down carelessly and squash a piglet to death. It happens often enough and if the piglet shrieks – and it will if it has wind for it – the dam gets frightened and mills round and round and maybe kills more as she does so. Worse, and this is most likely to happen with a gilt and her new-born fare, she will first bite the squealing piglet and then go on to kill the rest of them. If she were put to the boar again, we'd watch her behaviour very carefully, for infanticide might be stamped in her mind.

We'd always stop for a while if we happened by when a sow or gilt was in the process of farrowing. We put short litter in the pens and if she has time the female will bite it into even shorter lengths for her bed. In long-straw litter the new-born piglets may get their feet and legs caught and stumbling around, confused, they lose their way to the source of nourishment.

Part of the fascination of watching pigs born is the gamble of how many will be produced. The sow lies on her side and gives a quiet grunt as the first arrives. Then she is quite likely to get to her feet, look at the youngster and then, satisfied, lie down and let nature take its course as one after another the slippery little fellows, their ears stuck down fast to their heads, come sliding into the world. One hopes for a dozen.

The youngsters, each at first hampered by its own length of umbilical cord, go round the dam's hind legs to discover a teat – we called them dills – where they latch on fast and prepare to fight to stay there. Many times I've watched a whole litter suckling when after a time first one and then another ceases drinking and trots round to their dam's head and there is an exchange that looks a lot like 'Thanks, Mum' and 'That's all right, my child.' Fanciful of course but nice.

After farrowing, sows, if they can will always eat the afterbirth – the cleansings. But if Pinnock got there first he'd take a fork and throw them up into a tall hawthorn tree at the end of the yard. He'd been doing it for years. The branches were hung with the dry papery rags of old ones rustling in the wind, and fresher ones hung limp in slobbery swags.

'Why do you do that?' I asked. His reply didn't help much. 'Allus have flung 'em in a harva tree: my Dad done the same.' And he had nothing further to add on the subject. I could guess at a reason. It would be to prevent rats eating them, but when I suggested this to Pinnock he only grunted. Anyway, the practice of hurling afterbirth into prickly trees is an ancient one and common in many parts of the world.

Years later I read in the diaries of Parson Woodforde, the Norfolk cleric living in the second half of the 18th century, where he decorated the windows of a room with halva boughs to give them a Christmassy touch. I couldn't see winter hawthorn boughs making for decoration. It wasn't until still later that I learned that hulva, harva and hulver are all words for holly. I now know of Hulver Lanes and a Hulver Farm. But how it happened that hawthorn stood for holly in Norfolk and Essex is anyone's guess.

During my time at Justices the herd continued to do well in the show rings but I sensed that Euan was not so keen as he had been. This was noticeable when we went to a sale of pigs from a herd with blood lines which on past experience went well with ours. The

31

intention was to buy a young boar to put with some of the older sows.

The sale was held on a meadow with a tent where beer, coffee and sandwiches were available for the hoi polloi while the wealthier or better known buyers were invited to the farmhouse for pork pies, sloe gin or sherry. We were invited in at once. Euan was always accorded great respect at shows and sales.

The sale herd had a national reputation and there was a good crowd to hear the auctioneer extol its virtues. He had a national reputation too; he sold only pedigree stock and specialized in pigs and cattle, taking enormous trouble to know in detail the herd and animals he was selling. He had been known to refuse to sell an animal he thought failed to meet the standards laid down by the breed society. This gave him great authority and he was much in demand. Taking his position on a wagon at the edge of the ring he began.

'Ladies and gentlemen, you know my practice is to sell quickly and I'm not going to dwell.' (He notoriously averaged one lot a minute and was proud of it.) 'Start me then for Lot One, a promising gilt here, details in the catalogue, so start off for ten guineas, ten I'm bid, ten, twelve . . . all done at twelve then. Higginson twelve.' He was off.

We were seated, as was customary at farm sales, on tiers of straw bales. After perhaps ten minutes I started to itch. I scratched my ankle, then an itch on the calf. I gave that a scratch. Euan moved uneasily and rubbed his knee. Then I saw that all round the ring people, at first surreptitiously, and then openly – as they recognized they were not alone – were madly scratching themselves. In order to get at the source of the irritation

32

one lady exposed a length of thigh never before or after ever seen in public!

Bidding stopped. The auctioneer exchanged a few words with the owner and apologized for what everyone by now realized was a problem – lousy barley straw. Barley straw, particularly in some years, was notoriously liable to harbour lice. Although scientifically speaking I don't think they were really lice, the damned things bit just as well. The sale went on once clean wheat straw bales were put in the place of the barley bales, but Euan had had enough and we went home.

Once I arrived back at Justices from Chelmsford market to find Euan at the side door surrounded by a pile of tea chests. His father had died two years earlier and these boxes represented part of his estate. They were full of alcohol. Up until that day the cellar of Justices had had no more than a few crates of Whitbread pale ale, an empty cask, three old stone jars and a lot of spiders. For the rest of the afternoon Euan, Shinn and I carried case after case, box after box until there was hardly room for another. This was in fact the entire cellar of a very wealthy City merchant who drank the best. We spent ages sorting out ports, Madeiras, clarets, Burgundies, Moselles, hocks, brandies and liqueurs until the cellar became a cornucopia of alcoholic riches. The old man's benefaction extended further and the gunroom-cum-study where Euan did his desk work had stacks of cigars: more than twenty boxes of finest Havanas, some Churchillian in size, some short fellows pointed at both ends, some stout and short. The scent of cedar wood boxes permeated the house, sweetening the stronger smell of dogs, whisky and woodsmoke.

Not that Euan got much out of all this. As a youth in Australia he had acquired a taste for cheap whisky. He used to say he liked to 'feel it go down with its claws out'.

In an old-fashioned moral tale this ought to have marked the start of my descent into alcoholism, because Euan encouraged me to go ahead and experiment: 'Drink what you like, it is all good and won't hurt you if taken in moderation.' I don't know about moderation but I approached this educational opportunity with enthusiasm and thence forward drank at least a bottle of claret a week at dinner, with sherry before and port after. Brandy, Benedictine, Chartreuse, I tried them all. I ought to have fallen victim to the demon drink but didn't. I just developed a snobbish palate, which is now almost forgotten.

Cigarettes were a different matter. Euan smoked pipe and cigarettes alternately and always offered them. There were silver boxes of cigarettes about the house: Passing Clouds, Three Castles, Goldflake, Balkan Sobranie and so on. The brands were endless and the damage they did never ended either.

Chapter Three

Widening Horizons

ONLY two women other than the staff set foot in the house while I was there. Euan acquiesced in the case of a female cousin who made an annual inspection of the linen stocks and filled the gaps at the white sales. He neither knew nor cared how many sheets, pillowcases, tablecloths and napkins were wanted, but Mrs Whatsername did. Wear and tear in a household our size was light. I never saw a linen sheet that didn't look new. I was not to know how Mrs Whatsername managed the good lady – her name was Phoebe – but I know she had two linen cupboards and Phoebe looked in only one of them. This must have held ancient pieces saved from the very distant past all showing signs of wear. Each year, so I gathered, Phoebe bought large parcels of expensive linen which were tucked away with the previous years' purchases. Euan didn't care, but neither did he realize there was already enough unused linen to stock a small hotel.

One other lady did manage to get into the house while I was there. We were enjoying a Sunday morning beer, Euan reading the paper while I turned the pages of the *Farmer and Stockbreeder* when my eye caught a car turning off the lane and into the drive. 'Who's your lady friend in the chauffeur-driven Bentley, Boss?' I enquired. He walked to the window and looked out as the car slowed by the front door. One quick glance and scuttling towards the back of the house he cried, 'It's the 'orrible 'onourable. She's the Primrose League, the Lifeboat, the Conservative Association. I'm not in, I'm out and you don't know where I've gone!' The back door slammed as the Honourable's finger found the bell at the front door.

Having no instructions to the contrary I invited the lady in and played the deputy host, offering a glass of sherry, which was accepted, and a cigarette, which was not. I couldn't see any signs of a cloven hoof or snakes in the hair. In fact she was 'ordinary' and nothing to be scared of. She was, as Euan had guessed, looking for a contribution to the Primrose League. This sounded an innocent-enough organization (not as innocent as I was!) though why primroses needed support I couldn't think. They grew in profusion unaided.

'You people at Justices have always been very good. Primrose, Lifeboat, all worthy causes, wouldn't you say?' I hastened to agree and say that had Mr Lentner been here he would have done whatever was appropriate, but since he was not, I was sure he would wish me to find half a guinea on his behalf. This went down well. Perhaps I'd hit the right figure.

'Do you know, Mr Barrett (so . . . she knew my name), in all the years I have been calling here, only once have I seen Mr Lentner and that was in the distance. And each time we've invited him to dinner circumstances made it impossible for him to accept . . . a very busy man?' I confirmed that he was indeed an *extremely* busy man, and hinted at vast and complex affairs which took him from home at the most

36

unexpected and inconvenient times, and this meant social life was very restricted. 'In fact,' I went on, 'you could well say we have no social life at all!'

As we sipped and chatted her eye went round the room scrutinizing the furniture, the curtains, the pictures. Her expression altered momentarily when she noticed the saucy *Esquire* on the window table, not the sort of magazine she would care to open. However, having got into the house, which in her circle must have constituted a major victory, the good lady was patently anxious to get at least half a guinea's worth of first-hand information about Euan, his business and myself.

Her interest in Essex Saddlebacks was distinctly limited and of course I knew nothing of the Boss's business – just that there was a lot of it, so I came under her scrutiny. 'I don't think you come from near here? Your name though is familiar – perhaps your father . . .? My son Charles is at Felstead. Were you there in his time . . . he'd be younger than you . . . good at cricket. . . .'

This is the good old English game designed to find out whether you are within or without the pale of acknowledgeable acquaintance. There were a few more lightly made queries. 'Do you know the Hope-Mills at all – Hoxsneed Hall . . . Wimbrish family, awfully nice people.'

I know of no other country where one's antecedents, ancestry and status are so thoroughly probed. The process is so well practised and effortless that the victim is scarcely aware that his skin has been removed and his innermost parts subjected to examination. The middle-class country lady in her quiet tweeds, sensible shoes and healthy tan excels at it. This one did and by the time the interrogation had finished she knew maybe a little more about me than I was keen she should have. But nothing about Euan.

When he came out of hiding he quizzed me. That wasn't unexpected because although he didn't mix with the local gentry he liked to know what was going on and listened open-eared to such gossip as I could glean from whatever source it came. His social life was a vicarious one and I guess that in this I was an asset, for I went to places he never did.

And one of them was the tennis court at Worsett House, the home of my recent inquisitor. Euan received a brief note of invitation to play tennis in which I was included. This must surely have been a slightly mischievous stab for she can have had no illusion he would accept.

'When you see me on her tennis court – or any tennis court – send for a straightjacket. But you go. You've got flannels and so on and you can take the Alvis.' My car was a two-seater Morris with a dickey and not anything like as dashing as the Alvis Speed Twenty-Five. For himself he did not care, or appeared not to care, what people thought of him, but was patently concerned that I should make a good impression on behalf of Justices. He didn't say so, but I understood that the honour of the house was at stake.

On the day, sweeping down the rhododendron-walled drive in the Alvis, I arrived to find its status diminished by highly polished black Daimlers and Bentleys and an aged but opulent Silver Ghost. Worse, much worse, the tennis players, distinguished by their whites, or in the case of the ladies, by pale cream dresses, were with one exception at least twice my age.

And the non-players were even older with clerical collars predominating: two bishops of the suffragan kind, two canons, several rectors and a shy curate. Why on earth was I here?

I was to play in the first set. Myself and a late thirtyish lady – at a guess the curate's wife – versus an angular lugubrious gentleman, probably a disguised cleric who smote the ball with a will but into the net or out of court every time, and Ernestine, young, lovely and very good to look upon. She glowed: she winked at me whenever her unhappy partner smacked yet another ball out of bounds – and lost them the game.

We were halfway through a game when galloping across the court in pursuit of a ball which looked as if it just might land in our territory, I slipped and fell and in doing so greened my immaculate flannels on both knees. '*Oh, bugger!*' The spontaneous oath came out loud. My partner crimsoned from her face to the concealing top of her high-necked dress. Everyone, players and spectators, fell silent. There was not much I could do to retrieve the situation except try to cover up. 'Rugger . . . more like rugger,' I exclaimed, but I don't think anyone was taken in.

Then it started to rain and we were trooped indoors, giving our hostess the problem of what to do for the rest of the afternoon. 'Bridge; do you play bridge, Mr Barrett?' enquired one of the half-bishops as we gathered in the drawing room. Devil take my tongue! It would have been easy to say I did not, and leave it at that, but no, I had to add, 'The only card game I really play is strip poker. No! I mean stud poker . . . err . . . you know . . . with five cards' (this was the respectable game Euan and I played with an American who lived in

39

the village). The stark silence following this ghastly slip of the tongue was succeeded by everyone talking at once ... about anything, everything: the weather, church, state of the country (going to the dogs), and had anyone visited poor dear General Hawthorne-Logge in hospital. I was embarrassed, isolated, a pariah. Hence forward I'd be shunned by the respectable. My social goose was thoroughly cooked.

However, in the end it didn't work out badly at all. First, as I stood alone while the general horripilation subsided, Ernestine, my tennis opponent, came over and whispered, 'You've put your foot in it, haven't you? Golly! Language! I bet that word has never been heard in this house before.' She just kept from outright laughter as she looked at me.

I whispered back, 'Do you think so? It just came out ... and all these parsons. O God, it's awful!' Then in a firm voice she addressed our hostess, 'Neither of us plays bridge so if you don't mind we'll do a good deed and find the balls lost in the shrubbery.' Not waiting for a reply, she set off with me in willing tow towards the sombre gloom of the dripping laurels.

She was in charge. 'Too wet: let's go to the summer-house. You're Hugh. You are with that funny man at Justices, aren't you?' She rattled on. 'What do you do? Do you always drive that car? Bet it can go!' Inquisitive girl. 'All right, I'll tell you, but first, is your name really Ernestine?' She giggled. 'Yes, but everyone at home calls me Tut-Tut.' By now we had reached the bench seat in the summerhouse, and I asked, 'Why Tut-Tut?' She laughed. 'Because I complained to my parents that whatever I did they always said "Tut-tut", and somehow that became my name.'

40

I was smitten with her, and the attraction was mutual. Without speaking we agreed this meeting was not to be the only one and carried on kissing with increasing ardour until a call from the house put an end to our dalliance.

When I told Euan what had happened at Worsett House he almost choked between laughing and gasps of horror. 'Do you know what you've done? I shall never be able to hold my head up, never be asked to dine, play tennis or bridge or sit on the party platform. Do you realize half the county will be talking about it! Did you really say "bugger"?' And he let out another great guffaw, laughing until the tears ran down his cheeks.

It may be true that half the county heard of my fearful oath among the clerics, but instead of being banished, boycotted and cast out from decent society, the contrary was the case. Perhaps people were hoping for the thrill of a repeat performance but whatever the reason invitations to tennis parties multiplied. However, believing the chances of seeing Tut-Tut again were slim, I turned my back on tennis and concentrated on work.

Chapter Four

Lonely Farm and Departure

I'D BEEN at Justices for a twelvemonth and in that time the herd had done well at shows and the gilts we sold made good money. We'd won no Supreme Champion award, but more than a fair share of Reserves and Firsts. The Boss was pleased, Pinnock was pleased – for every win was reflected in his wages – and I was delighted because some of the credit rubbed off on me.

Euan had been talking to me about the litter-reared average we had been enjoying when he said, 'I've been looking at the calendar and see we're coming to a slack period: the Essex Show is not for weeks, nothing that matters much, farrowing for a bit. Good time for you to have a holiday.' I protested that I didn't need and didn't want a holiday: I wouldn't know where to go or what to do with one. He didn't respond to this but went on, 'You know that small man Mr Gimpson? He bought old Samson 2nd last year – before your time – sired some useful litters he told me. Not been at it for long but he's pretty shrewd.' I did remember him. He was thought to have only thirty sows, chosen with care as gilts, and with our Samson, bought cheap because of his age, was building a pedigree herd worth watching.

I also remembered Arthur Gimpson for a conversation he and Euan once had at the Three Counties Show. They were leaning on a hurdle looking at a pair of gilts which had just won a Second. Their examination had lasted some minutes when Mr Gimpson turned to Euan and rather apologetically said, 'Of course I don't know, Mr Lentner, but if the catalogue didn't say differently, I'd guess their pedigree is in their ears!' Euan looked about as if to make sure no one else had overheard this libellous suggestion, and nodded, 'Err, well hmm . . . yes. I have never seen ears droop like those – not on anything with a Burling sire, but it's not something I'd like to swear to in a court of law.'

The meaning of the 'pedigree in the ear' is broadly this. Pedigree animals were identified by a number consisting of nicks cut and holes punched in the ears. Reference to the herd book then gave sire and dam, so an animal's pedigree could be traced back for generations. An unscrupulous owner could assign an identity number purporting, perhaps, to show the animal had a sire or dam superior to its real parents. Essex breeders were generally conceded to be more upright than most, so it is possible Euan and Arthur Gimpson were wrong, as it can and does happen that a sire will throw progeny with widely differing characteristics – long ears, short ears, 'dished' face and so on. But serious breeders will avoid using them.

We got back to the question of my holiday. Apparently Arthur Gimpson had been confiding in Euan. He had to be away from his farm for two weeks, possibly a month or more, to look after his father in the West Country. Arthur, a bachelor, asked Euan if he knew of a herdsman who'd look after the place while he was away. 'What do you think? It wouldn't be a holiday, but it would be a change. I don't know much about his set-up but he says the house is comfortable. He'll pay a bit . . . what do you say?' I thought the experience would be useful and, although not keen to be away from Justices, said I would take the job on.

A week later at Lonely Farm Arthur Gimpson showed me round the piggeries, itemized his routines and the component parts of the various rations, pointed to problems which might occur, and off he went. So far as I could see this was such a well-run business that I had little to worry about. That was on the farm: the house was another matter.

Arthur was a bachelor. I had got used to living in a bachelor household, but not one like this. There was plenty of evidence in the shape of unwashed mugs, plates, cutlery, pots and pans, not to mention a heap of grubby clothes lying around, that Arthur was only semi-domesticated. In fact I doubt if he ever gave much thought to anything other than his pigs. I spent all the first evening cleaning plates and knives, forks and mugs, not a task I liked much, to get me started.

From then on I learned, what I had been told but had not experienced, and what hundreds of others had found out before me: that single-handed farming is slavery. There is no escape. You *have* to feed the animals twice a day, you *have* to see to their water, you *have* to cart straw and litter the animals, and prepare feed for the next meal, as well as feed, clothe and clean yourself and keep house. You do all this in baking summer heat, in freezing winds when the water pipes are frozen solid, and in snow when getting across the yard from meal shed to piggery with a bucket in each hand is hard graft. Seven days a week, three hundred and sixty-five days a year. No time off, no holidays, the pressure is to keep going and never let up. Of course it is slavery. The extraordinary thing to an onlooker is that so many people suffering this merciless, self-imposed relentless labour actually enjoy it!

For many, though, the real hardship lies in keeping proper accounts, the endless paperwork which gets put off or forgotten until it is too late. There are thousands of hard-working men, good at their job, who fail because the financial side of their business was at best a half-open book ignored for too long. Arthur Gimpson was not one of these. He had, as Euan remarked, 'More between the ears than was visible to the eye!' He must have, because he succeeded in keeping afloat during those hard times when so many did not.

I had none of these things on my mind when, having just finished an early last feed for the day, I saw a bicycle propped against the garden gate and perched on the wall, swinging her legs, the lovely, lively figure of Ernestine a.k.a. Tut-Tut. 'Bet you didn't expect to see me here, did you?' she called. 'Surprised! shocked more likely; wonderful, but how did *you* know I was *here*?' She looked pleased with herself. 'Oh, you know, one of the maids is a cousin to your Mona and I sort of found out. . . .'

We went into the house. She sniffed. 'Does anyone do the cleaning? Do you do it? The place is terrible, filthy, must be unhygienic and it smells of pig.' So it undoubtedly did, but in a very short time we had taken up where we had left off at the tennis party – only with none of the restrictions imposed by the possibility of parental or clerical interventions.

Although by modern-day standards we behaved with extraordinary restraint, Tut-Tut's mama would quite certainly not have approved, nor even imagined the speed and cheerful way her daughter threw off concealing garments. But truly there was little more than the joys of exploration with the unspoken hopes of greater joys to come.

All too soon it was 'Goodbye, goodbye!' as she cycled out of the yard. 'See you on Wednesday, but please, please get rid of that pig or I'll never come again,' and with that she vanished round the bend in the lane. She did come again, several times, and I did banish the pig which Tut-Tut disliked from the house.

This pig was different from the rest of my charges. The day after Arthur left I discovered her in a pen of gilts, sick and being bullied, as pigs will be, by her siblings. Her tail had been bitten to the bone, her shoulders

46

bloodied, so I moved her to a pen on her own. I fed her titbits of cabbage stalk, apples, stale bread and lumps of turf – an old remedy for dull pigs to root in. And as she ate I scratched her back, tickled her behind the ears and told her how beautiful she was – which after a few days of cosseting was true. Her eyes sparkled, her coat grew glossy, her frame was nicely covered and her disposition more affectionate every day.

It was not long before she got out of her pen and took to following me about the farm, snuffling and rooting for interesting things to add to her diet and probably cocking a snoot at her old enemies into the bargain. What I failed to realize was how attached she was becoming to my person. She wanted to be with me all the time.

She caught me unawares one day and jumped into the car as I was about to drive down to the village. This is when I should have read the signs and put a halt to the affair – but I didn't. I should say her name was Wellsden Grand Duchess III – a great and noble name, but she was not snobbish. She sat with me on the front seat and with her snout thrust forward through the open windscreen – for in those days the windscreens did open – she sniffed the wind, making happy little squeals the faster we went. She was fun and as good company as any dog.

It didn't stop at car rides. She took to coming back to the house at lunch and teatime, and finally supper as well. That was bad enough, but when she tried to follow me upstairs to bed it was too much. I smacked her hard on the nose, she backed away and had to make do with a night on the hearthrug.

Soon after I had left Lonely Farm, Arthur introduced

the Duchess to the elderly but active boar Dictator II, who had won prizes all over the country. In due course, so Arthur told me, she brought forth a litter of ten perfectly marked breed aristocrats, all potential class winners.

Despite a diet of bacon and eggs alternating with eggs and bacon, I enjoyed the Gimpson job. I missed the high living at Justices but felt achievement in having worked independently without trouble. And of course I had spent some hours of delicious torment in Ernestine's arms, tut-tut!

Euan was pleased I was back and questioned me closely about Gimpson's herd. I didn't mention Ernestine's visits and if he knew anything about the affair – and it would not surprise me if he did – he ignored it. Pinnock wiped the drip from the end of his nose and surprised me by saying he feared I might have gone for good. His dog wagged its tail and Shinn said 'Good morning' as if he meant it. Mrs Whatsername put on a four-course dinner during which I managed to shift a whole bottle of Burgundy. The return of the Prodigal was no better – and I'd been away for only six weeks!

I soon slipped back into routines which were really too easy. I was under-exerted both physically and mentally. Perhaps subconsciously feeling this, I persuaded the Boss we should increase and improve the cattle that were running any-old-how on the meadows. What started me on this exercise was the price of barley. Over breakfast one morning, between the egg and bacon and the ham, Euan said he could never remember barley ever being so low, as the price of Russian barley delivered on farm was in the region of £5 a ton. I bought a dozen or so cheap animals as stores, but I can't say my enterprise was all that profitable. Anyway by the time the cattle came off the excellent rough grazing on the meadows, not much barley meal was necessary to finish them off.

One odd thing sticks in my mind. The main cattle yard had a galvanized water tank with a tap above it. This tap had a poor washer and trickled non-stop and one of the steers, neck bent at what looked like a very uncomfortable angle, spent the greater part of every day sucking at it. The steer must have drunk at least twenty gallons a day, an aquaholic, and so far as I could see was none the worse for it.

The cattle were fine, the pigs were fine and I was fine too. So exactly why I felt an itch to leave I do not know. Euan and I got on as well as ever, in fact the longer I knew him the better friends we became, so my restlessness had nothing to do with him. I still got on well with Pinnock and Shinn and if I wanted company of my own age I had only to drive to Witham or Maldon to find it. Ernestine had departed the country and was being 'finished' somewhere near Paris. I missed her but not as much as I thought I would. No, I was probably suffering from too much ease, the symptoms being plain discontent. I would have to tell Euan I must move on.

I remember the day very clearly. It was a warm sunny Sunday morning and we stood at the top of the front door steps drinking pale ale and discussing whether to move the paddocks to a fresh piece of land. The present site, which had been in continuous use for a decade at least, was so infested with worms that even extra-routine worming had failed to eliminate them.

In the church on the far side of the moat, a service

was going on. A light breeze carried it to our ears, the dreary sound of a wheezy organ accompanying sad voices half a bar in arrears droning on and on. We listened for a bit. 'A very poor class of opium if you ask me,' said Euan sarcastically. 'If that makes life here more tolerable and heaven more certain, then God knows how or why. It beats me!' I put in a word for the Quakers, who were responsible for my early spiritual upbringing even if I was not a shining example of belief. 'Ah well,' said Euan, 'much better if they do without parsons and hold silent meetings and don't keep moaning on about their sins . . . Anyway, they probably don't have many to moan over!'

I couldn't see an easy way to say what I wanted, so I broke in with, 'Look Boss, I think it's time I moved on – ought to get some more experience. You did once say chaps ought to widen their experience when they can . . . and don't you honestly think I ought to move?' Euan did not speak for several minutes before saying we should discuss the matter over lunch. 'Think about it, no need to be in a hurry, think about it. I'd rather you stayed than went.'

But my mind was made up and during lunch we agreed I would stay on until my replacement was found. So that was that. But the moment the decision was made I began to have doubts, and went off to talk about it with a friend who might advise me. We met in a pub, had a few, and as we left he said, 'You are drunk, chum!' This was blunt but true. He saw me to my car and suggested that in the unlikely event I was stopped by the police or involved in an accident and hauled before the beaks I should simply tell the bench I had had a little too much to drink. He elaborated 'They

50

are all terrific topers and sympathetic to their fellow brethren, but speak up! They are all deaf as adders: my dad's chairman.'

Fortunately I got home safely but what he said about that bench was true enough. It was famous for having had a young man before it whose car had been badly damaged by a car driven by a young woman. She was denying responsibility while he was looking for reparation. The worthy old gentlemen listened for a while to what was being said but as lunch time got near, the chairman stopped proceedings saying they had heard quite enough: 'Shocking affair: disgraceful business!' A paternity order would be made out against the young man – ten shillings a week – until the child should attain fourteen years of age. The story as told to me ended thus, but would there be reasonable grounds for an appeal?

It took six weeks and many interviews before Euan was satisfied he had found a suitable new manager. He was a good lad. He didn't stay long, just a year, and quite soon after that Euan sold up and went to live in South Africa. He can't have been happy there because he soon returned and when war broke out he was appointed chairman of the county War Agricultural Executive, a job he did with almost fierce efficiency – turning down all pleas from owners of parkland that they should be spared the plough. I saw him only once after the war. He had bought a small farm and taken on a manager who was said to have 'robbed him blind' and according to all accounts he died a sad and lonely man. His birthday was 1 September and I always think of him on that day.

Chapter Five

Land Settlement

THE LAND SETTLEMENT ASSOCIATION or LSA was a government-funded organization set up to help long-term unemployed men become self-supporting smallholders. Substantial areas of land were bought and divided into smallholdings, houses built and would-be settlers taken on for an initial period of training. The men were recruited mainly from the north of England and Wales, and after their training they were joined by their wives and families.

I was lucky that within a week of leaving Justices I was taken on as assistant pig warden on a settlement near Colchester where the pig side had only just got started. The idea was that a sow herd would be established to provide each settler with weaners which they would fatten to bacon weight. That was the pig side; but there were also poultry units and of course each holding had land for horticultural crops – lettuce, tomatoes, onions and so on. Some holdings had glasshouses. Equipment – tools, machinery, seeds and feed – was bulk purchased and distributed from the settlement centre. The produce grown by the settlers was collected, bulked and sold on their behalf – a business managed by the settlement office. On paper the organization was thoroughly sensible, logical and well intentioned.

I lodged with Fred, an ex-miner, and his wife from Durham: I liked them although I found it hard to adjust to their ways, and particularly food. Justices was bad practice for living in a household where beef sausages – I'd not even known such things existed – were a bit of a luxury. And the tea from the pot which stood gently stewing on the hob from six in the morning until just before bed, by which time it would have tanned a horse and its hide, was hard to enjoy. Fred was short, stringy, tough, schooled in a harsh world and typical of most settlers, hard-working, independent-minded and very outspoken. His wife was equally tough but looked much older than her forty-two years. In many ways the wives had the worst of it in those desperately starved northern communities, nor did they find it easy to adjust to Essex rural ways.

I quickly learned from Fred and several other settlers that all was not well between 'the Office' and the men. Squatting miner fashion on his heels by the as yet empty piggery, Fred let off steam, 'Ah tell thee, them boogers at Office is robbing us, but thee watch, us'll fettle 'em! Some of our lads has heads on their shoulders and them'll see us right! They think we are fules, but we aren't so stupid as to believe them. They say, "Look here, it's down in black and white. You can't argue with that." But we can, you'll see.'

A row was brewing which fortunately had nothing to do with pigs. It was over the returns from the settlers' produce – lettuce – sold by the Office to Covent Garden or other of the big London wholesale markets. The settlers thought they were being done: there was a strong suspicion that the Office was cooking the books. For a time, settlers' complaints had been answered by showing them the market returns. On the face of it everything was above board: the prices returned matched the amounts paid out to settlers. But some settlers were still not satisfied. In great secrecy a whip round raised money for two delegates to go incognito to London and carefully note exactly what prices the settlement produce made.

A week later the settlers summoned the warden to a meeting where the delegates made their findings known. The market returns as shown to the settlers were compared with the prices observed in the market and they didn't match up. The figures showed that someone in the Office was conniving with the market salesmen to falsify the returns, and both parties were skimming a steady illicit income for themselves.

The settlers were jubilant. The meeting became a riot and the discredited warden retreated in haste. In due course he and some of the Office staff were sacked, leaving the settlers with the lesson that they had in future to look after themselves – and the accounts.

Considering the kind of people responsible for the LSA organization, it is not surprising that from the outset they failed to recognize that the North Country man, especially the miner, was entirely different from the rural East Anglian worker. Miners are traditionally both independent and inter-dependent: to survive they had to be. They had a sense of personal and corporative worth. They would not be patronized by anyone, least of all by the 'high-ups' in London or the Office, 'who can stop thinking they are distributors of charity'. As one man said to me, 'It's real men they're dealing with, not poor bloody Essex peasants.'

I had only been on that estate for a few short weeks

when the London HQ asked me to move to the settlement at Great Yeldham in north Essex which had more smallholdings and a larger central breeding herd. I was to be in charge. Just why I was moved and promoted remains a mystery, but it was welcome because a rise in pay was promised. Before leaving I asked Fred if he knew anything of the Yeldham estate. 'Aye, Ah knows some of the men there. Bonny lads − three from the same pit as us. They tells us it's no better there nor here. The natives gang to bed afore the hens: no life in 'em at all, man!' It was a common gripe that there was no social life − not even companionable drinking. 'Bloody poob shuts before nine and the chaps don't understand a word we say . . . no life in 'em, man!' Indeed there was no bridge across the north-south divide. That and the settler-staff relationship soured everything. And I had hoped to find Yeldham a more cheerful place.

Great Yeldham with its famous ancient oak was a quiet village whose rural calm had to some extent been upset by the advent of the LSA. Eighty-six new cottages spread out along the minor roads altered the nature of the village and eighty-six new and strange families with a different speech and habits tilted the balance of population very sharply. The central Office, warehouse, pig and poultry breeding units at one end of the settlement dominated the landscape − but not unpleasantly. I arrived just before Christmas and liked the look of it all.

The warden, Mr Crundle, greeted me. A big man in an open-neck shirt, rough jersey and cord trousers − a bit grubby − he impressed me. Here, plain to see, was a worker! His welcome was warm and he came quickly to business.

55

'Glad you got here smartly. In my opinion the pigs are not doing anything as well as they should. They've got to do better.' He had a deep, commanding voice. A touch of the sergeant major was my unspoken guess; it was confirmed in part when he continued. 'You'll find it a bit strange at first – new people, new methods. I did when I first got here: I was in the Australian Light Cavalry – nothing like this outfit I can tell you! Discipline. We have to have discipline.' This did not sound too cheerful to my ears, but his next remark did: 'They tell me you have the experience and the drive to get things done. That's what I want to see: energy and drive.' He gave such emphasis to driving energy I wondered who had given me this glowing reputation for I'd not been at the other settlement long enough to have earned it. Still, it was not unpleasant to hear that someone thought well of me – unless – and the thought did occur – I was for some reason being buttered up.

We chatted for a while about the problems I might expect to meet. These seemed to be centred on the settlers, or tenants as they were more properly called.

'They're a good lot on the whole, rough of course, but you'd expect that from northerners. There are a few bolshy ones you have to look out for . . . ignorant, trouble-makers you know, a few rotten apples. But any difficulty, any difficulty at all with them, you come to me and I'll sort them out for you. You can rely on me and my staff in the Office to help you all we can.'

I must say this rather worried me. It sounded as if he were anticipating trouble. All the time he was speaking he was looking me straight in the eye, which I also found vaguely disturbing and vaguely threatening: ridiculous of course.

The settlement breeding farm was well laid out, although farrowing was concentrated in two large buildings. I did not approve of this because in smaller units there is less chance of disease spreading. At a guess eighty holdings would each want at least twenty weaners a year – two lots of ten, but possibly more. A hundred sows should produce fifteen hundred weaners a year and since not all tenants had opted to fatten pigs, that should be enough. The pigmen – local chaps – were friendly if, I thought, dubious about having such a young boss.

The central piggery took up half my time and the rest I spent cycling round the settlement answering tenants' calls for help or advice. My job was to produce an unending supply of weaners for the settlers from the central piggery. As soon as they had got one lot of pigs to bacon weight, they wanted a fresh lot. So there was a lot of pressure on me to get good-size litters, and to ensure that they survived to weaning.

Apart from choosing fecund breeding stock, there's not much one can do about the number of pigs born, so it was a question of ensuring survival. Up until I arrived at Yeldham the average litter-reared number was seven or a fraction below. The generally accepted target at that time was eight. So my first concern was to ensure that conditions in the farrowing pens were as good as could be. I introduced farrowing rails to prevent sows squashing their infants, and creep feeds were put in too. These are a simple device which allow piglets to get at solid food but denies access to the dam. These, together with more careful and regular visits to the farrowing sheds, began slowly to improve results.

I found lodgings with Mr Seevers, his wife and daughter Evelyn. He was in charge of poultry. A comfortable bed, plenty of traditional food – joint on Sunday, cold on Monday, minced in shepherd's pie on Wednesday, sausages for Thursday and bacon, liver, eggs when all else failed. It wasn't up to Justices' standard but an improvement on the Colchester catering.

Mr and Mrs Seevers couldn't have been nicer. The daughter was the problem. I suppose she was in the awful throes of adolescence and fixed on me the full force of – to put it mildly – her affections. At mealtimes she managed to get her chair and herself so close that I could scarcely lift food to my mouth without finding her arm in the way. If I sat down in an armchair in the evening to read the paper, she would perch on the arm and ask me questions about . . . about anything that came into her head: 'Do you like Clarke Gable? What's your favourite colour? Have you got any sisters? Have you got a friend? Have you got a *special* friend?'

Now all this wouldn't have mattered, I regret to say, if she had been cheerful and happy. But she wasn't. She was miserable most of the time, and had a depressing habit of crooning an exceedingly sloppy song whose lyric contained the oft-repeated phrase, 'I've got my Love to Keep me Warm'. Wherever I went she was there too. In the piggery, on the tenants' holdings, or if I took a walk in the meadows or woods on a Sunday, sooner rather than later I would catch the melancholy strains of the song, and there she would be. Poor girl, she knew she was making no headway but couldn't stop trying.

In the end it was too much: I had to go. Mrs Seevers said she 'understood' and dared say she was the same at that age. I moved into the house of an elderly widow close by the Great Oak. A comfortable bedroom, a sitting room to myself and the good widow cooked and brought me my meals to be eaten in solitary pleasure. It was in fact quite luxurious. The charge, which included laundry, was 30 shillings a week. Coal was 6 pence a day. I was being paid £4 10s 0d a week, so I had over £2 to spend. Being near the White Hart, this was not a problem. I acquired a taste for draft Bass.

For two months or so everything went swimmingly. I got on tremendously well with the tenants and the staff pigmen were okay. Then came a series of difficulties.

Once a fortnight I ordered the feed necessary to keep all the breeding stock at the centre going for the following two weeks. The calculations were not difficult. It was simply a matter of knowing how many pregnant and how many farrowing sows, or sows with young; how many dry sows and boars; and then how many pounds of mixed feed for each per day. A matter of simple multiplication to work out the total requirements.

The bother was that while my arithmetic, done and re-done many times, seemed right, it didn't work in practice. Days before the end of the fortnight the pigmen came telling me we were running out of feed. We checked the weights and measures used. They were all right, so I told the men to cut the rations a little and see what happened in the next period.

In the meantime I had a meeting with Mr Crundle and told him of my difficulty over balancing the feed equation. I then came to the matter of the weekly birth reared numbers.

I was enthusiastic. 'It is rather good, I think. I am just one piglet short of having the average reared come to eight. Now I've got some good litters almost ready to wean, so I will "borrow" just one of those pigs for this week, because I'm positive we shall hit the eight thereafter without any trouble.'

'*Would that be cricket*, Barrett?' he demanded. 'Can't you wait a week to show how clever you are? For God's sake . . .' He looked me straight in the eye as he said this as if accusing me of the grossest malpractice. I can't say I felt the least guilty, but he had managed to hit me where it hurt for I *did* want to be known as good at my job and I *was* rather cocky: not so much with the tenants but with the staff.

I couldn't think of an adequate response. If he considered 'borrowing' one paper pig wasn't cricket – I couldn't honestly see where cricket came into it – so be it. I couldn't match his moral tone and walked away feeling hard done by and cross.

The next week found me in more trouble. The pigmen reported that we were short of heavy iron feeding troughs, and the wire I had ordered for some outside pens wouldn't go the distance I'd calculated. Then a number of new feed buckets were suddenly missing. I reported to Mr Crundle. He scowled and said, 'I expect we've got some light-fingered settlers at work. I'll have a look round. For the moment don't say anything to anyone. Leave it to me.' That suited me and I went away almost but not quite content. I didn't really believe we had a thieving settler – nor for that matter did the pigmen behave like crooks.

At the end of the next fortnight period I found we were even shorter of feed than before and I went again to the warden about it.

'You'll just have to cut the rations again, or . . .' and he paused, thought for a moment and went on, 'perhaps you should order more.'

'I don't want to do that. I've calculated what is needed and it ought to go round and perhaps have a hundredweight in hand for emergencies – a tenant might run out or something.' The warden grew red in the face.

'Ah, so you've been passing out feed to settlers then, eh? That's strictly against the rules.'

'No, I have not given anything to any settler, and there's nothing wrong with my calculations.' And feeling extremely angry I went on, 'If you don't believe me, get your clerks to do the calculations and see what they find.'

At this he went an even deeper red and shouted, 'Are *you* telling me what I should do now?'

Mildly I replied, 'No, not at all, I'm suggesting. . . .' But my suggestion got no further.

'Well, you can take your suggestion back to the pigs then!'

I really couldn't see how we had arrived at this situation but it was a row which ended quicker than it had begun. 'No, thank you very much,' said I, mounting my high horse, 'I am going to resign – *now*!' And I stamped over to the Office to give them an address to send my cards to. As I walked out Crundle stormed in, but if he was about to ask me to stay or to speed my departure, I shall never know.

I pushed past him and started back to my lodgings, wondering where I had gone wrong. On my way I talked to one tenant – Will Williams – who raged about the organization and the way tenants' complaints were ignored. I listened as he sat on his heels and spoke.

'We had this meeting at t'weekend. Jones and me got to tell everyone how we reckoned *we* never got the weight of food they charge for – I reckon two pound a month we paid too much. Then the charges they put on for selling our eggs. Too bloody much, I tell tha. Anyway, everyone was shouten and hollerin about it, but old Crundle somehow he pulled t'wool over their eyes. We wanted to call in the London people, but he persuaded them he would look into our complaints himself – and that's where it stands now.'

'Are you happy about that then?' I asked.

'No, Ah'm not. But that Crundle . . . he's a tough booger. Make you think black is white. Us don't trust him: well, Ah don't.' I couldn't make any constructive comment. That was the last conversation I ever had with any tenant.

Later all was made clear. With the help of the clerical staff, Mr Crundle had forged my receipts and had taken a farm some miles away which was found to be stocked with LSA equipment – including pigs, 'my' feed, buckets, troughs and wire and heaven knows what else. He was sent to gaol. They had also forged my salary slips at six pounds ten shillings, thus earning an easy two quid for themselves.

To end the story does not take long. Yeldham and many other of the settlements more or less emptied shortly after the outbreak of war. The tenants went back into industry where the earnings were more reliable. A very few stayed on, but gradually the holdings were let on a commercial basis. Today, some are still working as co-operatives, but I doubt whether any of the original families who came down from the north or Wales can be found.

In a short history of the LSA movement it is acknowledged that they found great difficulty in getting staff of the right calibre. I would not dispute that, nor that any staff could have been more trusting and naive than I.

Chapter Six

Finchingfield

AFTER shaking the settlement dust from my shoes, I had enough cash in hand to stay on in Yeldham for a few days.

Every evening I went to the White Hart and drank enough Bass to justify keeping a bar stool warm. On the fourth evening a man who seemed vaguely familiar came in. He ordered a drink and asked, 'Hugh Barrett, if I'm not mistaken?' I remembered – Kenneth Read, a few years my senior during the short period when we were fellow students at the old East Anglian Institute of Agriculture. A short, rubicund, curly haired man who favoured silk cravats, sheepskin coats, open cars and a long cigarette holder, in order words, very 1930s. But I liked him – he was amusing and if he had taken his studies and the authorities lightly, so had I.

We remarked on the smallness of the world and he asked me what I was doing. 'Having a quiet drink and wondering why you choose this moment to disturb the peace. What brings you here?'

'Me? Well, I farm not so far away and some evenings pop in here for a meal. Being a bachelor I get bored with beans on toast and the farm can look after itself for an hour or two.'

I joined him in a very good mixed grill – half a crown

– and we chatted on. 'I've told you I farm, but you – in agriculture, I suppose?'

There was something about Kenneth (who constantly quoted, or misquoted, Dr Johnson) that made our conversations wordy and sententious. I replied, 'Yes, certainly in, or as it happens just out of, agriculture, having recently resigned from a position of great importance in the locality. I am now actively considering what to do next to further my career and improve the lot of my fellow citizens.' I don't doubt we went on in this way for some time.

Kenneth told me how he had bought a farm on the outskirts of Finchingfield – reckoned by some to be the prettiest village in East Anglia. One hundred and fifty acres or thereabouts of poor light land for which he'd paid £7 an acre. A small, early sixteenth century timber-framed house, decent barn, stables and sundry lesser buildings.

He described it at length in glowing terms and by the time that 'Time, gentlemen please' was called, it was agreed that I would join him and perhaps, if we got on well enough together, I would add my small anticipated inheritance and we'd be partners in an enterprise and become the envy of the county.

The next morning I packed my bag, thanked the widow, mounted my bicycle and pedalled the rolling miles to Passmoors. Kenneth had not exaggerated. It was a charming farm in ageless, beautiful elm-clad landscape: very romantic.

The house stood a hundred yards back from the road down a rough, stony drive that widened into the yard. A thatched barn and stables stood at one side and the house set in a small garden was on the other. Originally the house had been thatched but it had been peg-tiled some time in the 1800s. It was like thousands of other timber-framed farmhouses and buildings in the region – nothing exceptional. They look as natural and as much a part of the landscape as the trees and meadows around them.

The land was poor light sandy stuff. Not so good but not very different from Home Farm where I'd been a pupil. The weeds which flourished – plenty of the pungent-scented stinking mayweed (*Anthemis cotula*) – told that the soil was acid. That was something we could cure in time with heavy applications of chalk or lime.

It was in the early 1930s that a great change in acid and light land farming began. Research and practical demonstrations carried out in particular by A.W. Oldershaw on the sandlings of Suffolk showed how through the use of lime such land could be made profitable. It started a revolution.

There were literally tens of thousands of acres in East Suffolk which were held as sporting estates since they would grow nothing worth ploughing for. Earlier in the century huge areas were sold for as little as ten shillings or a pound an acre for the game shooting. Mr Oldershaw, whom I knew and greatly admired, introduced the practice of liming, which together with his advocacy of planting cocksfoot and clover leys and lucerne, which were fed off by sheep, changed the style and profitability of farming. In fact, although it was years later, light land, especially where irrigation water was available, became as dear as good productive heavy land, which is much more expensive to cultivate.

I remember that spring and summer as idyllic. We

worked hard and enjoyed it. I'm not sure how long Kenneth had been in possession but it wasn't until I arrived that we bought – or rather were given – a horse. Euan gave us Gypsy – the broken-winded mare which had lived outside and done only the lightest work at Justices for years. Gypsy was a honey. Heaven knows how, but her wind was no longer broken, although broken wind is believed an irreversible condition. She was the most willing horse I'd ever known. In the morning she'd come at my call from the meadow and straight into the stable to be groomed, fed and harnessed.

She positively *enjoyed* work and best of all she knew what was expected of her. Put her in the horse-hoe shafts, set her off between the beet rows and after a few bouts she would, without a touch of the lines, turn on the headland and be ready to start off again in the correct row. She also walked neatly between the rows so didn't tread on the plants.

At Home Farm I'd once driven a pair of Suffolks abreast in a heavy harvest wagon up Princes Street in Ipswich, right over the Cornhill and beyond without using the reins. Words of command sufficed, and Gypsy understood 'Coopi wi', 'Wurdi', 'Jisstep' and 'Back-a-bit' as well as they had. And she was strong: never jibbed however heavy the load. She was one of the rare horses who would go almost to the knees to shift a stubborn load.

We grew sugar beet – eight tons an acre wasn't reckoned too bad on that land at that time; today, you'd expect maybe eighteen tons and more. Wheat, eight combes an acre, barley about the same. In other words, nothing to boast about. Nor ultimately were our livestock results any better.

There's an old saying that 'One boy's worth half a man, two boys no man at all' and I have to be honest and admit that two men like Kenneth and myself were probably worth half a good man. We worked, worked hard even, but not consistently, and if a test match were being broadcast on the wireless Kenneth had to listen. He was himself a first-class club player and nothing could keep him from it. It was an infatuation, a disease. Another more fundamental factor was that Kenneth had no urgent need to work at all. His family had the sort of money found wanting in mine. Anyway, neither of us, after the first few months, could be described as farming in deadly earnest. There's a lesson in all that which does not need spelling out.

We enjoyed life. Despite there being no tapwater – pump in the yard – and cooking and lighting were by oil, we were comfortable. Kenneth bought an old iron bath and put it in an outhouse which had a wide fire-place. We put a faggot under a copper and then ladled the hot water into the bath. Drying in front of the still blazing hot fire was sheer pleasure. So were the lunch-time bread, cheese and beer at the Fox – and the evenings spent in the small back room there. The land-lord had a hen which loved beer. It would hop on the bar and wait for someone to stand treat. It must have had a good head. I never saw it drunk.

I wanted us to go in for pigs, Essex for preference. I bought three females, a gilt for twenty-five pounds which was really too much; a sow that had had two litters for ten pounds; and a non-pedigree sow in rather poor condition for four pounds ten. They were all sold as in-pig. For the moment that's where we stuck and awaited forthcoming happy events. There was plenty to do. We worked in the sugar beet, horse hoed the wheat (surely one of the last times that operation was performed?), repaired buildings and started on the inside of the house.

It was while we were doing the ceiling at the top of the stairs that we noticed a square mark in the old plaster which, when chipped away, revealed a trap door leading into the roof. We scrambled up. The roof space ran the whole length and breadth of the house, with the solid brick chimney in the middle. Most of the area was open joists but yard-wide boards ran from the trap door to the chimney, which had a sort of boarded platform about six foot wide round it nailed to the joists, and on it an old sack of straw, a bowl and a pail. Three or four foot above the boards there was a heavy chain circling the chimney. We speculated about what this was for but came up with nothing credible. Later we did learn.

One morning a man with a travelling stallion was walking with his charge past the roadside meadow where Gypsy, in season as it happened, was grazing. The leader, a stubby little man who must have been nearer seventy than sixty, brought the stallion down the drive to ask if we wanted our mare covered. I don't believe we had ever thought of putting her in foal but it didn't seem a bad idea: in fact what nicer than to have a foal on the place? No thought given to the fact that we should for a period lose the use of our mare for any but light work, or perhaps, since she was far from young, we might perhaps lose her in foaling. In short, the romantic cut out the logic.

There is no more gallant and magnificent sight than a

rampant stallion covering a willing mare. Tail and mane braided with coloured ribbons, coat shining as a polished chestnut, the briefest of preliminaries and the beast rose with flashing hooves as Gypsy stood to him and the act was over. I remarked to the leader what a fine and stimulating sight it was.

'Yeah, an' you ain't the fust to feel it neither.' He paused for a few moments and went on, 'Back twenty year or more ago I come here every year. They had a mare . . . no, they had two, and time I were here with my hoss they fetch out a gal fer me. She used to watch and then we went inta the stable. They took her indoors after, and a' course I never charged 'em nothen fer the stallion. I done it like that several year.' Kenneth and I were literally struck dumb: what could one say? Nothing. It was too gross, and as if in some obscene medieval story, the man marched off with his stallion leaving us speechless.

'See ya in three weeks, but I reckon she'll have took,' he called as he left the yard. (There would be a free second service if the mare returned in season.) We hoped not to see or hear of him again, and since Gypsy proved to be in foal, we never did – other than as he walked the roads.

Sadly we had to believe this story was connected with our find in the house roof. Several people subsequently told us about a man and wife who lived at Passmoors some time past, and said they were thought to have a daughter although she was never seen.

'They kep' her out of sight, some say tied up: a bit touched – you know – innocent like.' That chain became sinister in our minds, the word in this case being horribly appropriate. It was said the couple stayed only a few years and then went away, no one knew where.

Such happenings seem incredible today, but I suspect they were common enough in isolated East Anglian villages a century ago. Even during our time, tragedy was not far away.

Kenneth and I were mending a roadside fence one evening when a twelve-year-old lad, the son of a neighbouring farmer, halted for a moment. He was leading a cow which he'd taken to another neighbour's bull. He stopped, obviously wanting to say something and suddenly came out with it. 'Ain't you heard?' he asked.

'Heard what? What about what?' said Kenneth.

'My dad done hisself in this morning. Hung hisself in the barn. Done it with binder twine. I'm taking th'old cow home now.' And he walked on. All this had been delivered in a flat emotionless tone. He spoke as if father hanging himself was as much a part of an ordinary day as taking the cow to the bull. The boy told the truth. His father had committed suicide in the horribly memorable and different way from the shotgun or horse-pond suicides so common among farmers in those run-down days.

We had wonderfully good weather for harvest that year, but woefully poor yields. I don't think we bettered eight combe an acre on any of the three fields growing wheat, so traving (in other places better known as stooking or shocking) and carting were made light of.

We had the help of my art student brother Roderic and his friend Picton. Neither had ever done harvest work before, but Picton found this so satisfying that he almost there and then decided to leave art for agriculture.

After the day's work we hopped into the Austin Seven two-seater and rushed over to Bardfield where there was a good deep swimming hole in the river. Off with our sweaty shirts and headfirst into the water. It smelled faintly of cows. We swam round for a while luxuriating in the cool. Then out, into clean shirts, and off to the Fox for long pints of beer.

Talking of cereal yields, we used the word combe. It was spelled variously, coomb or coombe or combe, but it had a specific meaning. Originally it meant four bushels – a measure of volume – which was one sack, the combe sack. Later the combe was given weight values. Thus a combe of wheat weighed eighteen stone, while a combe of barley, that grain being more bulky, was fourteen stone, and oats a mere twelve stone. Two combes are equal to a quarter, which was the quantity in which prices were usually quoted. Today everything is in hundredweights or kilos and it is illegal to put up grain in sacks any heavier than twenty-five kilos. Not a bad thing either. Try carrying eighteen stone (two hundred and fifty-two pounds or, curse them, one hundred and fourteen kilos up granary steps! We did and if it did us no immediate harm I'm sure it did us no good either: too many spine and hip joints ultimately damaged.

Four acres of wheat proved unsaleable. It was contaminated with a wild onion whose bulbils were about wheat grain size and could not be dressed out from the threshed grain. Worse, many bulbils fell to the ground and grew. The result was we had a field whose produce stunk of onion. No merchant would touch it and how we got rid of it I don't remember: perhaps fed it to pigs or poultry. The onion was probably *Allium oleraceum* or *A. vineale*, crow garlic. We tried to purge the soil of it by sprinkling paraffin where we could see it germinating. A pious hope doomed to failure.

The pigs were doing nicely. The expensive gilt on which I lavished undue attention looked splendid, the ten-pound sow burgeoned, and even the four-pound-ten ancient had filled out. She had a good temperament and in a pitying sort of way – deeper emotion for a four pound ten animal would have been improper – I rather liked her.

One can never be absolutely certain about farrowing dates but the time came when the gilt was due. I looked at her last thing at night and first thing in the morning. As soon as it was light I'd put on a dressing gown and go to her pen. It is the best time to be about; the sun not yet above the horizon and the birds beginning to stir. Blackbirds start their 'spink–spink' and an early green plover calls in the distance. The air has a fresh, clean, unused taste. . . .

After a number of these night and morning trips to the gilt she started to farrow. I stood quietly watching. Everything was normal as the first piglet arrived and made its determined way to the teats. Good! A fine, healthy looking lad. I waited. Five minutes I waited, ten minutes, and then with a grunt she expelled the afterbirth. *Twenty-five pounds and only one blinking pig to show for it!* I could have killed that gilt with pleasure. Not only had she made a financial loss for us, but, and this hurt more, it was as if she had deliberately set out to make me look an idiot in the one area where I was certainly most experienced and knowledgeable.

The ten pound sow farrowed the next night. She produced seven and then cleansed as I watched. Everything seemed all right and I went in to bed. Next morning I looked in on her. Four piglets were suckling, two lay flattened on the floor – the farrowing rails had not saved them – and the seventh, also squashed, was gasping its last.

I failed to see the four-pound-tenner farrow. She did it unseen and produced and actually reared thirteen to weaning.

We sold the gilt's single animal as a suckling pig at three weeks to a London butcher – it might have been Fortnums, for Kenneth had contacts in that direction. It fetched several pounds. Hoping that it was just by chance that things had gone so badly, we mated all three females again, but apart from the old cheap sow who went on producing good litters, they were useless. I had left Passmoors by then but I was told the local butcher bought the gilt and put her head, an orange between her jaws, in the shop window. I could with pleasure have stared her straight in the face.

Kenneth, as I have said, was mad about cricket. He had a portable wireless – heavy old accumulator-powered thing – which he moved up the rows as he worked hoeing sugar beet. It slowed him up but that didn't matter too much. What bothered me was the amount of time he spent *playing* cricket. Every week-end had a bite out of it, and sometimes there was a mid-week match where he was needed. He played among other teams, for Essex Gents – for this was still during the time when there were 'Gentlemen' and 'Players' – two quite distinct categories.

Kenneth infected me slightly with the cricket bug

and once carted me off to Southend to watch a match between Essex Gents and Essex Doctors. The gents *had* to be short of a player. I was togged out in someone's spare flannels and as last man went out prepared to knock up a few sixes. It was actually more cock-up than knock-up: middle stump first ball.

Cricket meant that I was often left single-handed on the farm. I didn't mind that too much, but Kenneth had the Austin and I was left with my bicycle – frequently flat tyred – or Shanks's pony to get to the Fox. It was a downhill ride going and uphill coming back, so I usually walked. It was a pretty walk, and in the summer that year glow worms were more plentiful than I'd ever seen – or seen since. I had stopped and was bending down watching these creatures on the roadside verge when the owner of a nearby cottage came up and made himself known to me. He was C. Henry Warren, the first author I had ever met.

He invited me into the cottage and offered a drink saying 'Sorry, I can't give you sherry because I've sworn not to buy a bottle, nor drink the stuff until the war is over and, God willing, the elected government is reinstated.' He was speaking of the civil war then raging in Spain.

It is a sorry confession to have to make and I can only think it was that I read no newspaper, rarely listened to the wireless and Kenneth had no political convictions, that the Spanish war had not touched me: not at that time. But the intimations of 1939 did. On that same 'glow worm evening' Henry turned on his powerful wireless set and it happened to be broadcasting from a Nazi rally in Germany. I shall never ever forget the thousands of voices crashing out 'Sieg Heil,

Sieg Heil' time and time again. Senseless, mindless, mind-shattering roar of the mob that disturbs me to this day.

Henry and I remained friends from that time up to his death in 1966. I had always thought he was just a few years my senior, but he was older by twenty-one years and had fought in the First World War – a fact I learned only from his obituary in *The Times*.

Finchingfield like all villages had its share of mental cases. Generally inoffensive, just occasionally 'difficult' and sometimes hard to tolerate. Kitten – I never knew his proper name – was one who was liable to turn off the road he habitually tramped and walk down to the house where he'd stand staring at, so far as one could see, nothing in particular. He was a handsome man and I'm sure would never hurt a soul. The Arab saying 'A well-populated head is a sign of a cultivated mind' would if taken literally suggest that Kitten must be brilliant. Get within two yards of him and the livestock was visible running from his tangled red head down to his neck and back again. This infestation must have been exceptional, yet I never saw him scratch! The village accepted him, almost tolerated him, and I suppose he was happier than if he had been in an institution.

One week Kenneth had been away for two days. I'd coped with the stock, arranged for five acres of stubble to be ploughed by a helpful neighbour, and of an evening cooked and eaten cheese soufflé, a dish I was good at (much depends on the quantity of water per egg). I went into the sitting room to read.

This room was thirty foot long. The heavily beamed ceiling was higher at one end than the other. To get under the low end if you were taller than five foot six called for a humble attitude or a cracked skull.

All the timbers – and it had plenty – were black oak which made the room dark too. A wide brick fireplace big enough to take six foot logs was at the east end of the room. Dark panelling flanked it on both sides, and a panelled door led to the narrow stairs.

At the other end there was a door leading into a passage which in turn led to the kitchen, dairy and boot room which was shorthand for the place where we chucked boots, dirty clothes and hand tools (a good place to lose things).

The evening wasn't cold but I had a few logs burning – for company more than warmth – and sat in a high-backed Windsor chair. I lighted the paraffin duplex lamp, set it on a small table slightly behind me and started to read Darwin's *Voyage of H.M.S. Beagle*. I was soon engrossed in it but after perhaps five or ten minutes I heard the sneck of the door latch slide down so that the door could open. Holding my book open in one hand I got up, shut the door and returned to my chair. A few minutes later I heard the sound again. I got to my feet and this time made sure the latch was firmly pressed into the sneck. Obviously, I thought, I hadn't secured it properly the first time. Back to Darwin, but I had by now what might be called a trembling ear. I half expected that door to give a repeat performance.

I was never given to over-speculation about the cause of inexplicable events because nine times out of ten one finds a logical explanation in the end. So I thought of the various things which might have caused the present phenomenon and concluded that notwith-standing my care I simply hadn't done what I thought I had. But in this case I failed to be convinced by my own logic and when the door latch sounded again I became distinctly uneasy. So much so that I half turned my chair so that I would see if the door opened, which it could do because I could see from where I sat that the latch was unfastened.

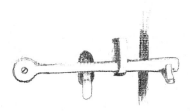

The door stayed just ajar and I gradually relaxed. I had got to the part of the voyage where Darwin describes the miserable state of the Tierra del Fuegans when a whole section of the fireside panelling fell out and crashed to the brick floor in front of me.

My God! I jumped to my feet, dropped the book, picked up the lamp in such haste that the draught blew it out and scrambled through the door, upstairs and into my bedroom.

I was scared, frightened, and for all I told myself there *must*, of course, there *must* be a reason, this did no good at all! Miserable coward, it was only in the morning hours that I fell asleep.

Downstairs in the morning I carefully examined the door latch. It was in perfect working order. The panelling lay where it had fallen and I examined the wall where it had been attached and the panelling itself. Clearly it ought not to have detached itself: no reason at all. So what? I don't know, but my thoughts did turn to what may have been the unhappy spirit of a mental girl chained to the chimney breast in the roof. When I told him about it, Kenneth immediately convinced himself this was the case. There being 'more things under heaven and earth', I am content to leave it at . . . doubtful.

Gypsy needed shoeing only once while I was at Passmoors but it led to my knowing the blacksmith. I don't know what his surname was as he was always referred to simply as Sam. It was a pleasure to take the mare into his smithy. There are places which nearly always make me feel cheerful. Whether it is the rhythmic roar of fire as the smith pumps, the bellows, the sparks flying in the smoky air, the hammer ringing on the anvil or the pungent scent of burning horn, I don't know. Combined they create in my mind some antique memories and I feel happy and content.

Gypsy was quiet and patient. A touch on the fetlock and she lifted a foot: no need to heave and pull. She knew what was required of her and obliged. This gave Sam opportunity to talk. He owned an elderly large white sow, an animal he doted on. He took me to see it. If memory serves me well, he called it Peggy. Peggy lived at the bottom of his cottage garden furnished with a comfortable sty set in a small wooden-railed pen. She was large, heavy in-pig, and about as healthy and clean as a pig could be.

'She looks well, Sam,' I said. 'What do you feed her on?'

'Nothen, only middlings. That's all she get, middlings.'

I was shocked. 'You can't feed a sow, especially an in-pig one on nothing but middlings,' I explained. 'She'll do no good on that.'

Sam stroked his chin and perhaps weighing up whether what he would say might offend, said, 'Well, sir, I expect you're right, but she's six year old come Michaelmas and she ain't never had nothing different – 'cept bits of kitchen waste an' I chuck in a turf and a bit of coal now and agin.'

Those last ingredients were quite commonly given to pigs kept indoors or in places where they couldn't get at grass. It did them good: or we thought it did. In due time Peggy pigged and Sam called me to have a look at her. There she was, on her side contentedly suckling a litter of thirteen. Sam said, 'She had fourteen but there was one real weak one; not a runt, just weak and cold. Didn't want to lose it so we took it into bed, but blast! That got overlaid in the night. Dead as dead! But there, sir, she's got enough left, ain't she?' And with a sly sideways glance at me innocently added, 'Middlings if fed right do all right!'

It has since struck me that at the time I saw nothing exceptionally out of the way in Sam taking a piglet into the matrimonial bed. I had heard of it being done before. Nothing on earth is cleaner than a little pig. But I also have to say that Sam and his wife were not lightweights and the outcome might have been foreseen.

It is impossible for me now to put a finger on the exact reason why Kenneth and I parted company when we did. I had been at Passmoors from spring drilling to autumn ploughing and in all that time we had had no disagreements serious enough to have words about. There were the problems of cricket, but perhaps the underlying difficulty was the difference in our financial situations. I really do not know. But whichever or whatever, we parted friends and remained so up until his death.

After I had gone, Kenneth moved out of the house and into the pub. I fear he drank a bit. Then without warning he ceased farming, entered theological college and in due time ascended the clerical ladder to become a canon and abbey chancellor.

As for me, I had long years to go before I deserted the land. In the meantime, unexpected and unplanned, my career swerved abruptly off course.

Chapter Seven

Sylston Park

NEVER take on a job without first doing some research into what it actually entails. I had put an advert in the *Farmer and Stockbreeder* and almost before the ink was dry, a North Country voice over the telephone invited me to manage his 600-acre estate in Lincolnshire. Of course I said, 'Yes, when do you want me to start?' 'As soon as tha can – tomorrow if tha like.' (Note: He didn't question my qualifications.)

Two days later I got a lift from Grantham station and was dropped at the South Lodge gates of Sylston Park. The woman lodge-keeper answered my knock. I asked if this was the right place. She responded with a question, 'Are you the latest manager then?'

'I hope I am the new manager but why did you ask if I was the latest?'

'They coom and go. They don't last long,' she replied. 'Us had one a fortni't since. He walked oop t' big house and were walking back through these gates inside of an hour. He didna last long, did he? Nor the man afore him!' She delivered this information with a perverse, pitying pleasure.

A more than faint suspicion began to creep into my mind. 'Well, why don't they stay – why such a short time?' She answered briefly with a cackle, 'They's in too much of a hurry to stop and tell me. Th'd best wark oop t' big house and find out!'

The drive ran alongside a lake of about ten acres dotted with small willow-clad islands, then sharply uphill past clumps of huge old Spanish chestnuts. There were noble oaks and elms and a few conifers. Halfway up the steep hill, I stopped to rest for a few minutes at a handsome marble basin, which was a horse trough. Water trickled in while Neptune overlooked some sportive lifesize nymphs dabbling their toes below. Very fetching.

At the top of the hill – three hundred feet above the Lodge – the land flattened, and following the drive round through a wood and then a shrubbery, I found the house. It was almost a mansion. Over the front door was a truly enormous oval marble plaque – five feet across – carrying a coat of arms and an extremely long Latin inscription. It looked much too big for the house and I found out later it had been bought at a demolition sale.

Even more out of scale were the adjacent stables, huge, and topped by a crumbling ivy-clad clock tower which reared above the surrounding trees. Once it had all been very grand indeed. Now it had the still beauty of a romantic half-remembered past. But the romance of the decayed grandeur and beauty of the landscape ceased when reality in the form of my new employer appeared. He was, as he variously described himself, a 'no-nonsense, straight-talking businessman'. 'Say whata-mean, mean whata say; you be straight wi me an' I'll be straight wi' thee.' He was short, rotund, with a very red face set in a pear-shaped head. He was a dealer and doing nicely – shiploads of railway lines, thousands of tons of grain: anything to make more 'brass'. His biggest deal he boasted was some shiploads of canned sardines which he bought in early '39 and sat on until the war sent the price sky-high. So he was in a fair way of business – if that sort of business can be described as fair. But, and there was no doubt about it, he was also a lunatic and not an amiable one. It didn't take long for this to become abundantly plain.

His name was Skeggs. The estate was about six-hundred acres, ringed by a ten-foot-high stone wall, the only entry points being by two lodges and a chunk of wall felled, so I was told, for the convenience of a royal fox-hunting duke.

There were pieces of woodland originally planted as pheasant coverts and a sixty-foot-deep stone quarry – two acres of it where rabbits and badgers lived. In a far corner there were fifty acres of arable land. The rest, parkland, provided grazing for nine horses and a flock of Ushant sheep, a breed unknown to me and, so far as I can tell, to everyone else. They were small, black and looked after themselves, and a herd – or perhaps collection is an apter word – of around forty Dairy Shorthorns made up the rest of the livestock. And a more miserable lot of craggy animals it would be hard to imagine.

The staff was *one single solitary worker*! How does a manager manage a staff of one? The question hardly arose. Mr Skeggs decided what should be done each day and a wondrous business it was too. He knew nothing of farming beyond what he picked up from his Liverpool traders and it can't have been much. So what happened was that Jack (the staff) and I did what we could. He did the ploughing – it was late autumn – and he did his best with the cows. These were a major problem. It was my good fortune that only a dozen were in milk while I was there.

The cowshed, close by the north lodge gate, was equipped with a milking machine, but I doubt if it had been cleaned and disinfected for months. The in-milk cows were riddled with mastitis. I had watched Jack drop the suction cups into the gully and pop them back on to the udder. There was no time for the niceties of dairy hygiene. Why the local milk depot accepted the stuff can only be put down to the blanket excuse for everything – the war. The milk collection lorry had to come right past the gate but Mr Skeggs believed the driver sold some of the milk to other farmers before it reached the depot, so he ordered the churn should be taken in by 'the staff' or the manager in a pony trap! Crazy. I did the trip several times myself and was hugely embarrassed to see the yellow and red streaks being tipped from our churn. It was ghastly. But there was no time for hygiene and the idea of calling in a vet to treat the various bovine ills – and mastitis was only one – was promptly stamped on. 'Ah've got no time for fancy vets, thankee!'

Among the rest of the cattle, abortions were commonplace. It was nothing strange to see a fox slinking off across the park carrying a foetus away to the woods. There were scores of foxes all performing this useful sanitary function.

Alongside the upper end of the main drive there were two wheat stacks. They had been held over from the previous year and never been thatched. For what reason I cannot imagine, the order went forth to thresh them. I did suggest that it might prove an expensive exercise because the stacks were sodden. But he took no heed. So the tackle arrived with three men and we began to throw the sheaves down to the thresher.

It was a slow job. The straw was so wet it bunged up the screens and there was almost as much water as wheat going into the sacks. We persevered, throwing the worst and wettest to the ground rather than attempting to thresh it, and at the end of the day – eight hours' work – we had exactly nine sacks of totally unsaleable corn.

The threshing tackle man said he'd had enough and took himself and his machinery off. I told Mr Skeggs the result of our efforts – nine sacks, I said. Next morning he swore we had threshed ten sacks, and where had the tenth gone to? He wasn't this time quite accusing me of stealing a sack of wet wheat but I had the impression he would have liked to.

The second stack stayed untouched and just got wetter and wetter. So much so that when during an air raid one of a cluster of incendiary bombs landed on it, it failed to catch fire.

I really don't know why I didn't throw in my hand much earlier than I did. Perhaps it was partly not wanting to be beaten (which I was!), partly feeling it would be unfair to leave Jack single-handed again, and partly because whatever else, the park was so overwhelmingly beautiful it almost made up for the awfulness of the rest.

Things were so bad, the work so demanding and impossible to do, that after a long battle I managed to persuade Mr Skeggs to take on an extra worker. And I knew just the man, Picton, my old friend who now knew much more than I did of cows. So at last I had some company at work and a chance in the evenings to exchange views on the subject of Skeggs and all his works.

Picton and I shared an uncomfortable unheated cottage – it may have been the laundry house – and a kindly woman came in to cook one meal a day. Skeggs wanted to charge rent but I baulked at that. As time went by he became more and more unpredictable and acutely paranoid. He had a morbid fear that everyone was stealing from him. Fat chance anyone would have had. Everything was locked: the barns, the oil sheds, even the stables.

He ordered and counter-ordered. I'm sure he fell only just short of certifiable. Jack told me that he ill-treated his wife and the only time I saw that unfortunate woman he was bullying her and she was in tears.

There was one comic episode. One afternoon he invited me to 'Coom oop t'house for a drink after sooper.' I accepted. When I was seated in front of a roaring coal fire with a glass of whisky in my hand, he self-approvingly commenced, 'Ah cud see t'war were coomin. Ah've a hoonerd ton a coal in t'cellar. Us'll not go cold – tha'll see.' And then with no more ado he handed me a small volume of poetry. 'Tha's a good voice. Ah want thee to read a bit of poetry.'

I was stunned. 'Err, which poem do you want?' I asked, not able to fetch up a sore throat at such short notice.

'It's by the *great Lakeland poet*,' he said, giving heavy emphasis to the words. 'Tha'll find it on page thirty-three, called "We are Seven".'

My family has ever faced challenges with courage and fortitude! It required all these and more to keep a straight face on hearing this demand. So I read a bit flatly at first, but warming to the task, gave the verses that measure of sentimental syrup appropriate to them and my listener. As I finished I looked up to see Skeggs, overcome by an excess of emotion, wiping the tears from his eyes. Under other circumstances it would have been quite touching. He sighed.

'Tha read that joost loovly,' he said. 'Just loovly.' Fearing further demands I made excuses and hurried away.

Not all such events were so innocent: some were sinister. One morning he came out to me in the yard. 'Get thy gun. We'll have a goo at rabbits in t'quarry.'

'Oh no!' I protested. 'I can't do that, I've arranged with Jack to finish the wheat drilling: he's ready now.' His face grew a deep red.

'Oh ah, and who pays thee a'Friday then? Let Jack get on alone, he've done it before. Thee'll coom wi' me.'

Weakly I did as I was bid, fetched my gun and went with him to the quarry. He had brought six or eight ferrets which I suppose he looked after himself, for I'd no idea there were any on the place. He loosed them at the bottom of the quarry and then stood alongside me on its lip. The ferrets sixty foot below went to work. We stood watching. I was silent. I was angry and besides that, rabbits won't bolt if they hear noise outside.

'Ah reckon thee'd like to push me over t'edge,' he said. I did not say the idea attracted me, and moved a couple of paces further away from him, trying to look as if I hadn't heard. 'Ah'll tell thee. When I die there's a moonth's wages and fifty pun for everyone working for me. What do tha think of that?' I was not amused. He sounded in dead earnest. Not funny at all: I really thought he was inviting me to help him into the next world and said nothing.

It was not this however which finally tipped the balance. Skeggs had got more than coal hoarded. There was a very large barn packed to the roof with linseed cake, decorticated cottonseed cake, fishmeal, bone meal, as well as wheat and barley. That barn – more the size of a small hangar – contained hundreds of tons of scarce animal feed and particularly the near-unobtainable high protein stuff. When and where he got it all I don't know, but it was illegal to hold it.

It was a Friday night. I had gone to the house for my wages. He thrust the cash – about a fiver – into my hand and said, 'You're sacked. I won't have any spies on the place. What good did it do thee to tell t'War Ag about the barn stuff? You're a sneak and I won't have it.'

I was naturally furious. 'I've told no one. I don't know anyone in the War Ag and I'm not sacked, I've bloody well resigned and if you do get copped I shall not be sorry.' With that, as they say in melodrama, I swept out shaking with rage.

Next morning I trundled down the drive, kissed the nymphs on the way and hitched a lift to Grantham in a Bren-gun carrier. I had been at Sylston for less than four months, but what an education!

Thirty years later I went back to Sylston again. The stables with the clock tower had vanished as if they had never been: not a stone remained. The park railings were gone, and the house was empty with broken windows. A door hung from broken hinges. It all bore the hallmark, the imprint, of some get-rich-quick farmer–entrepreneur. There was money in land and none in houses at that time.

The short-cropped grass of the park had gone under the plough, the woods had been raped for firewood and the quarry enlarged. There was one reminder left of how I saw it first. Neptune was still looking on at his delicious full-bosomed nymphs as they sat round their faintly greening bowl washing their delicate marble toes in the trickle of spring water. It was very touching to see such pure sensuous figures left unravished. Perhaps someone about the place had a soul after all. What happened to Mr Skeggs in the short term I have no idea, and for the longer? I must be charitable and, like the Arabs, say that the Almighty looks after lunatics, however undeserving.

The Bren-gun carrier dropped me in Grantham and I caught a train which in due course arrived at a station near my home. Seventy miles in ten hours! That was wartime travel.

Chapter Eight

Shropshire

I WONDER how it was that my father accepted my rapid changes of employment with such equanimity. He was not what could be called a worldly man, but he knew how the world ticked and must have noticed that whenever I got a foot on what looked like the promotion ladder, it slipped off sooner rather than later. If he did notice, he said nothing. How wise.

The truth is that between the ages of seventeen and twenty-two or three I changed employment so many times in so many different places that Father probably didn't know at any given time exactly where I was. Yet whenever I turned up at home to tell him of my next move, he always said, 'Yes, that sounds a good idea, give it a try. Why not?' And like as not changed the subject to denounce the Tories or capital punishment or any other of a score of issues about which he felt quite strongly.

Two things he said when I was about twenty have stuck in my head. 'Boy, if you want to make money, buy and sell things. But if you want to be happy, make them.' The other was, 'If anyone offers you a return of twenty per cent on your money, you can be reasonably certain that if there is twenty per cent to be had, it'll not be you who gets it!'

Why he produced these dicta I have no idea, for I never dreamed of leaving agriculture for anything else. I was in any case legally obliged to stay on the land as a condition of conscientious objection to military service during the Second World War.

The incredible Judge Hargreaves presided over the Appeals Tribunal in Fulham court where I was summoned to appear, and he dismissed my ethical arguments as redundant. 'You are already working on the land – a reserved occupation – so unless you are thinking of changing, don't waste my time. Go away and don't bother us further.' It was this judge who said to one appellant, 'God isn't a pacifist, he kills us all in the end.'

I had gone to Sylston Park with no more thought than it takes to eat a banana. With just as little thought, I took a train to Shropshire where the post of assistant manager of five hundred acres was provisionally offered to me.

At Stone Farm an elderly housekeeper showed me into the office of the owner, Frank Laye, who hastily ended a telephone conversation. 'Yes, yes, sorry, got a man waiting. Call me later,' and wasting no time he shook my hand and started the process of discovering if I was the right man for the job.

It didn't take long. Overlooking my youth and inappropriate education, and without telling me much about the farm or giving me a chance to ask questions, he ended the interview abruptly. 'Have a go, try it out. See how you get on, Hugh – all right if I call you Hugh? Don't mind? Good. Don't know much but you'll pick it up. Tomkin will put you right. Good, I'll see you next week!'

I got used to it in time but he was like a tightly coiled spring about to fly. He rarely spoke a real sentence – just bites of words which you had to be quick to get the drift of. He farmed very hard indeed. Always in a hurry, impatient: like a terrier anticipating a rat hunt and not wanting to hang about waiting. He was a goer.

I lodged with the farm manager, Tim Tomkin, at Kirk Farm and I found my way there at once. Tim was a tall, lean, stringy man whom I correctly judged by his accent came from Essex. Mrs Tomkin was round, jolly and pink and blonde with many more words than her husband. They made me welcome and while she was getting the supper ready, Tim told me about the farms – for there were two – and my duties. It was a shock to find that during parts of the seasons my principal job would be to 'look after the women'. Noting my indrawn breath and expression of alarm, he kindly added that they might seem difficult at first. 'They are not like the women in East Anglia – but you'll find out. They're all right really.'

The farms were given over almost entirely to horti-cultural crops – large-scale market gardening: carrots, turnips, parsnips, cabbage, savoys, kale, beetroot, early potatoes and green peas. There were tractor drivers, a few general labourers (these were the days before 'labourers' became 'workers' or 'craftsmen') who did the basic cultivations, and with them was a very large almost permanent gang of women. I didn't know too much about women as women and nothing whatever of them as fieldworkers.

My gang was made up of twenty women: some young, some married, some not, some middle-aged and one or two grandmothers. All were regulars and had been doing farm work for most of their lives. Not just the light jobs – hoeing and such – but muck carting and spreading, harvesting and haysel, jobs where strength counts.

Tim took me out and called to their leader, Mrs Collins. She looked at me and I looked at her in a brief summing-up, and then I offered my hand. A girl in the background said, 'Coo, nice manners ain't he.' Another, amid giggles, commented 'Nicer looking than the last feller.' And this was followed by remarks of a more personal nature which I didn't quite hear but suspected were not so complimentary.

I had arrived when there were acres and acres of carrots about four inches high, and my first task was to organize the work of thinning and weeding them. I had to allocate each woman a row. The work was done mostly on their knees using a short piece of stick to scratch out the unwanted plants and weeds. Locally it was aptly called scrawling – and a tedious job it was. I tried a hundred yards or so and decided female backs bent easier than mine.

It was all straightforward until the mid-morning tea break. 'Here you,' sang out one of the brawny girls, 'what's your game then? Look at what you've set me – rotten dirty weedy row when you give Hilda a clean row and shorter too.' Then another called out, 'She's right, he don't know fair from friendly, do he. Got your eye on Hilda, haven't you! Yeah, we know your sort – overgrown schoolboy!' 'That's right,' shouted another, 'and don't think you can play any games with us. We know our rights.'

It didn't matter whether they were widows of sixty, young married women or single girls: they all knew

how to get at me, and my ears that day and for the first week were perpetually red. Nowadays it would be described as sexual harassment. How I suffered!

They were dressed for work in drab woollies and thick skirts. They would have to wait another ten years before fashion hit the fieldworkers. One woman was different from the rest: Mrs Taylor, a gypsy, who lived with her husband and infant in a caravan at Kirk Farm. She wore a high-necked, close-fitting long black dress with a two inch gold medallion at her throat. With her olive complexion and black hair, she was as exotic as if strayed from the Mediterranean. She neither spoke nor was spoken to by the others and didn't join them in ragging me.

Those women had my measure. It wasn't too bad when one or two of them felt cause for complaint, but when twenty or more had the same grievance and came up to me in one furious body I often wished I could hide.

'Ladies!' I cried. 'Please listen for a moment. . . .'

'No, you listen to us, we're not ladies, we're honest

working women and we won't be put upon. Just you come and measure those rows again.' This from Mrs Collins was backed up noisily by the rest until I agreed to re-measure their work. What a shout went up when they found I was a yard or two out! They hooted and jeered and laughed and called me names. One strapping young woman said, 'You make that mistake again and we'll get you down and gnaw your knees!' And I'm sure they jolly well meant it!

Yet in time we rubbed along well enough. I probably got a bit smarter and saw that half their pleasure was in putting me in the wrong. But the fact is that I simply didn't have the faintest idea of how they ticked. Nothing in my life had prepared me for this.

They had been quick to suspect that I favoured Hilda, a quiet, slow-moving girl with a nice smile. I liked her because she was quiet and for nothing else. She, poor girl, had every reason to be slow. One Thursday she failed to turn up to work. I asked Mrs Collins why she was absent. 'Why? Go on, tell me you didn't notice . . . her's having a baby, any fool could tell that.' This fool hadn't, although I had noticed she walked a bit heavily. Poor Hilda! She was back at work on Monday and wearily came to me and said she was sorry she had had to miss Friday!

'How's the baby?' I asked. 'Is it a boy or a girl?'

'Didn't they tell you? It was twins but one was born dead.' Whatever she may have been feeling she showed no more emotion than if she had lost a kitten rather than a baby.

'Are you sure you should be working, Hilda? You do look rather pale . . . I mean oughtn't you to be looking after the baby?' I felt responsible; she was, so to speak, one of 'my' women. But no, Hilda felt all right, thank you, and her mum was looking after the children. 'Children?' I queried.

'Yes, I had two last year: they was twins too, boy and a gel.' I could think of nothing to say to that and walked away uncomprehending.

The farms were on an area of deep old sandstone south of Shifnal. I have never seen land like it. Free draining, fertile and incredibly easy to work. I'm not sure whether it was of any real benefit, but they used a single-furrow Melotte plough which regularly turned a furrow three foot deep. Deep ploughing was fashionable. The theory was that you ploughed a little deeper and brought up some of the subsoil each time. Then through cultivations and weathering it was incorporated and became fertile topsoil. Occasionally the Melotte got its point under a piece of solid sandstone – usually eight inches or so thick and the size of a large table. These then had to be hauled off to a bit of waste land where in time I expect they were broken down by rain and frost.

The gypsy Jack Taylor and his wife and infant lived on that corner of land in their traditional horse-drawn caravan. Jack, a savagely handsome, black-haired, red-neckerchiefed man, was a part-time horse dealer who travelled about the country in a high dog-cart with a very fast nag in the shafts. He drank, was quarrelsome, but rather admired for the furious pace he drove and his contempt for everyone not a Taylor. He had class.

I never knew what his wife was called, nor saw her infant. She was a regular and when one morning she didn't turn up the rumour was that her child was ill. The doctor's motor had been seen by the caravan. The next thing we knew was the child had died. The women clubbed together to buy a wreath and everyone felt sorry for Mrs Taylor.

Two days later the women were seething. Everyone wanted to tell me the dreadful news. The Taylors had set fire to their caravan and burnt it and, so everyone said, the entire contents, to ashes. I saw for myself the still-smoking embers. All that was left were the iron tires, the cast-iron stove and melted brass and glass. The women regarded this as wanton vandalism and were horrified.

'All the bedding, the kid's clothes, ornaments – I seen in, and they'd plenty,' said Mrs Briggs.

'That's right,' chimed in Hilda, who could have done with some infant clothes for her own. 'It's wickedness, heathen wickedness!' The Taylors, along with others of their semi-nomadic kind, were totally alien. They were thought capable of casting the evil eye. It was not this, though, that infuriated the locals but the destruction of good stuff – tangible wealth, property – the ultimate sin.

In some ways it was a good time to be farming since almost anything grown would find a market. There was a four-acre field of vegetable marrows and for at least a month a young man by the name of Walter Yarrow was all day cutting and barrowing marrows to the road-side. If there is such a thing as the world's worker, he was it. He was always called 'Pity' because he so often uttered the words 'Pity me!' Whatever he did – hoeing, sprout picking, cabbage cutting – he did at top speed. He would never take day-work. It had to be piece-work. To this day I've never seen anyone set out cabbage plants so fast. I asked him if he liked piece-work (a silly question) and he said, 'Piece-work, of course a'do. I can earn twice as much than at day work. I'd pick me nose piece-work!'

The marrows which he cut and carted were collected twice a week by a large furniture van. The driver told me he was delivering them to an airfield for the NAAFI. 'Well, that's something,' I said, 'they must eat marrows day and night to get through the loads you've taken.' 'Not likely, mate. They don't eat a tenth, not a fiftieth of 'em. I backs my van into the old hangar each time and shovel them out in front of the load I took the time before. Stinking squelchy mess worse than rotten cabbage!' To be 'in' with the NAAFI was a very desirable state for a farmer. The amount of corruption was substantial. Very wicked, of course, but a welcome change from farming through the depressions of the twenties and thirties when nothing you grew was wanted.

I several times told Frank Laye that apart from measuring up at the end of the day, I need spend little time with the women – they knew the work and better than I did. 'Yes, that is true,' he replied. 'But you stay away most of the day and see how much less work gets done – even if it is piece-work. And weeds will get left, work skated over. No, you keep on.' It was rather boring.

One day the work did seem to have been slow and jokingly I said to Mrs Collins, 'If you lot worked half as hard as Pity does, you'd have finished this field last week.' She looked at me and called to the others who were packing ready to go home. 'Come you here and listen to what he say. He tell me we ought to work like Pity do.' I protested that was not really what I meant at all, but Mrs Collins knew she had me cornered.

'Ah, you say what you like. I know what you meant all right. I'll tell you we don't work like he do because we don't have to and he do!' This was getting me a bit confused. 'Why does he have to work so hard then?' Mrs Collins looked sideways at the gang who were enjoying the argy-bargy, and then, waiting for a few moments to give weight to what was coming, she said, 'Young Pity's a proper feller. Mad with girls he is – you ask Ivy here.' 'Pity,' continued Mrs Collins, 'is a married man with two kids of his own and two his wife brung with her.' I said I could understand that to support a family like that called for hard work. 'Tha's nothen, he's paying for a little boy in Shifnal, and there's a paternity against him in Bridgnorth. Work! He work day *and* night.' At this the girls giggled. Even Ivy, whose connection with Pity I could only guess at.

It was patently true that nothing would curb Pity's amorous urges. During haysel a girl pushing a pram with a baby walked along the road past where the gang were eating their midday 'snap'. When she was out of earshot someone said, 'Now do you watch what she's up to.'

The girl shoved the pram across the field to the far side where Pity was resting and handed him a packet of sandwiches. The women were goggle-eyed to see that once the sandwiches were finished, Pity and the girl vanished into the ditch, leaving the pram on the head-land. It was obvious Pity was showing his gratitude in the way he knew best.

Lodging with Tim and his wife was successful. We got on well together. But there was a snag; there always is. It was fleas. Mrs Tomkin was a thoroughly good housekeeper. The broom, the duster and vacuum cleaner were in constant use, but I'm positive neither she nor anyone else could have stemmed the tide of fleas which found their way into the house. They came from the thousands of hessian bags brought from London to pack the produce in. Why these bags should be so infested I never understood. We had exactly the same problem at Home Farm, although there the fleas stayed in the barn – or most did.

In the yard outside the back door a stout post had been concreted in. It was free-standing and was used by Tim and Frank Laye, but especially Tim after breakfast. He came out and putting his back up against the post, shifted up and down and sideways, giving a good and enjoyable back-scratch. I got in the habit myself. It countered the itching flea bites.

Coming in at mealtimes we'd sit down and within minutes the little beasts hopped from the carpet and made their biting way up our legs. It happened every day and nothing, no flea powder, paraffin or Jeyes fluid, had the least effect. I never went to bed without a cake of soap to stick them to. But my nights were always troubled and I got asthma attacks as well, which didn't help.

In the end the asthma attacks got worse and made me less than effective and I decided to leave. In addition to my work with the ladies, I'd learned something of the planning which is essential when growing a wide variety of crops, getting them harvested and sold and carted away. It was a complex problem which took in dealing with markets, market prices and transport firms; even railway timetables had to be considered. It was the co-ordination of growing, marketing and transport which had to be meshed in order to make a smoothly working business. Taking part in all this was good experience for me which came in useful later on.

Frank Laye was emphatic that he didn't want me to leave. We got on wonderfully well, as indeed I did with the Tomkins, but I reckon, although they never said so, that they must have had enough of my wheezing.

I said goodbye to my ladies saying I was going to miss their company. For their part they didn't express any very deep sorrow but offered to provide me with all manner of outrageous carnal delights should I decide to stay. But with heartfelt thanks for the thoughts, I said I had to leave.

Hilda was pregnant once more, Ivy was more than halfway along the same road, but now being married she was beyond gossip. I never returned but remember them all with slightly qualified affection.

Chapter Nine

Refugee Camp

M Y AIM after leaving Shropshire was to go to a farm in south Norway owned by a very well-known pig breeder, as I wanted to top up my expertise and Scandinavia was the place to be. The Danes and Swedes in particular were leading the world in bacon production and I imagined Norwegians were as good.

I had a month at home before I was due in Norway and in this time I was reintroduced to life and events a long way from the plough.

My father had been active in securing a place for Basque refugees near Colchester, and following that he was among the Quakers and others in supporting a camp just started for refugee Jewish children. It was in Dovercourt close to Harwich. Father suggested that before going to Norway I could help at the camp. So I volunteered and was accepted.

My first task was to organize sufficient hot water bottles – and the hot water to fill them – for the many hundreds of German and Austrian children in the chalets, for this was a summer holiday camp and it was now winter.

That was just a beginning. Every week hundreds of children – boys and girls, from four to sixteen – arrived at Parkeston Quay. I remember one boy whose back bore all the scars of a severe beating. He was very quiet about how this came to be. Whatever the age, they came carrying all their worldly possessions in paper parcels or pathetically small satchels. Their passports were stamped with a large capital 'J' for Juden; all the girls' names had been changed to Sarah and the boys to Jacob. Everything the Nazis could do to humiliate them was done.

The camp was always full and as more arrived those already there had to be moved and places had to be found for them. Some went to relatives here and in America; many were taken in by concerned Jewish families. Quakers and other religious people took numbers, and as is always the case in Britain there were people who had no sort of connection with Jews or religion but who felt compelled to give homes to children in distress. Some children were shipped to a colony in Paraguay.

Some children were fostered, others adopted outright. Decisions had to be made, and made quickly. No doubt some foster-parents and adopters were not well matched with the children they were taking into their homes. There cannot have been any very detailed enquiries. There was no time.

On Sunday the children stayed in the big hall, walking about, playing or just sitting, while the would-be fosterers weaved their way among them looking for one to fit their requirements. It looked uncommonly like a slave market and the fact that pretty little girls (preferably blue-eyed, we cynically noted) found homes soonest bore this out. Fifty years later I met a number of these children and heard that on the whole the system or lack of it had worked. Most settled in their new homes happily enough. Some did not. There were cases where children were forbidden to speak their native tongue. Some were 'converted' to Christianity. But whatever their situation, as knowledge of what was happening in the concentration camps got out, they suffered increasing awareness of their parents' plight. None escaped some degree of lasting trauma. Ultimately most lost not only parents but other relatives as well.

Under pressure the camp could house seven hundred, and that is what it did hold: a changing population of seven hundred children to be fed, clothed and kept warm. What made it more difficult was keeping these children occupied and as happy as circumstances allowed. They had been torn from their parents and were fearful of what was happening to them and of their own future. It was not easy.

The logistics of an ever-changing situation, of keeping hold and of grasping situations as they developed, had to be faced. When I got there the camp leader was a very impressive elderly lady, Anna Essinger, who had a school, Bunce Court, in Kent. She managed somehow to shape and weld the ad hoc collection of young British, mercurial Viennese and more dour German staff – none trained for the task – into something like an effective organization whose difficulties were compounded by the fact that so many volunteers were there only during academic vacations.

The atmosphere in the camp was always charged with emotion, some days worse than others. The worst were when news from Germany arrived. The good days were when fresh supplies came in – donations from firms like Marks and Spencer, who sent pantechnicons full of clothes. They sent more hot water bottles, gumboots and food. A large ham was one of the unexpected gifts and the Gentiles among the staff cheered at the thought of a delightful change from horse. That ham didn't quite turn out to have their exclusive attention, as it sorted out the kosher from the rest.

I had two particular friends who came into the latter category. They were both medical students, Max Evnine and Harry Winner. Both had come to England from Russia around 1920 as refugees from the excesses of the post-revolution period.

I visited Max's home several times and was fascinated by his family. Father, mother and the two sons were polyglot. I doubt if inside the family they ever managed a sentence in a single language. They were equally at home in English, Russian, German, French, Yiddish and Hebrew and used all of them indiscriminately. Mealtimes were a babble for they were passionate about almost everything and didn't hide their feelings.

I made an unsuspecting remark in that household. The Evnines were not very orthodox, and Max least of all. His parents thought, however, that he had strayed rather too far from the ancestral fold. On hearing that at Oxford Max had enjoyed bacon and eggs, his mother cried out 'Maxy! Maxy! Not bacon. Think of your father, your grandfather. Think of your poor aunts. Not bacon, Maxy, I beg you!'

I had a job keeping a straight face. He, I'm glad to say, was unregenerate. It was during one of my visits that I enquired whether a dish on the table was kosher. This made for a misunderstanding of my religious convictions, for some days later Max's mother said, 'Max, why don't you bring more *good Jews* like Hugh home?'

I had achieved honorary Hebrew status by accident – at least in that household.

The pressure of work was such that if an opportunity to relax came, we grabbed it. One evening Max, Harry and I, together with one or two more, went into Dovercourt for a meal at the best hotel there. It was so good to get away from the camp with all its tensions and sit down to a blow-out – which is what Harry inelegantly proposed it should be. The food was ordered and soup on the table when the waiter said there was a call for us. It was from the camp asking us to return quickly because a rumour had spread that a pogrom had started in Vienna.

We dropped our spoons and rushed back. It is impossible to describe the situation. Imagine seven hundred contagiously frightened, crying, wailing children all milling about the huge and echoing dining hall. The Viennese staff, poor souls, were in almost the same state. They knew better than the children what a pogrom meant. They were caught and held in a state of total panic, some quite hysterical.

We tried to get news of what was happening in Vienna. London apparently knew nothing. Lines to Vienna were blocked as were those to Berlin. Finally, and it took the best part of an hour, we made contact with Vienna by way of Czechoslovakia and learned the rumour was false: there was no pogrom – not at that time.

Then came one of the most moving experiences of my life. It was not going to be easy to stop what had by then become mass hysteria. Shouting above the noise was hopeless, as it could even have made matters worse.

Then in the middle of the hall one of the older

Jewish helpers began to sing. First, almost as if to himself, a Hebrew hymn, known even to the youngest there. The hymn was a message of hope and courage in adversity, and the effect gradually spread. Another adult took it up, then another, then little by little the ripple grew wider as the children joined in. My hair literally stood on end: there was something almost unearthly about such poignant, passionate emotion. Even today when I think of that moment when the wailing ceased and the singing took over, my heart misses a beat or two.

The winter of '38 was a bad one to be housed in summer chalets. At Dovercourt the sea actually froze and one night when high tide and winds combined to break the sea wall, the lower part of the camp flooded. We had to turn out and carry the children through thigh-deep freezing water to safety. I had my reward three days later when I coughed and coughed until it hurt.

Fortunately a wonderful nursing sister, young but trained in the old school, came to look at me. 'Bronze sputum!' she exclaimed, a euphemism for spitting blood. Sister Bush had me into an ambulance and in the Cottage Hospital in double-quick time. There I was given the new wonder drug M & B and a clammy kaolin jacket, and within a month I was back with the refugees once more.

Not at Dovercourt, which was now closed, but at Barham House – an old leper hospital, a pest house near Ipswich complete with a mortuary, cells and a grave-yard. It was a spooky place in daylight and much much worse at night. It housed only a hundred or so boys. I found there were plenty of helpers without me.

So I left and returned to the land. I never did get to Norway and that was probably a good thing, for the farmer, I later learned, turned out to be a notorious quisling and I might have been cut off in Norway during the war.

Max Evnine died in Italy during the war. Harry Winner became professor of pathology at Charing Cross Hospital. We remained in friendly contact until his death in 1993. Sister Bush married and we corresponded for many years.

As for the children, who would now be in their sixties and seventies, all have disappeared from my sight.

This brief period had a greater effect on my later life than I could have imagined at the time. It certainly changed the way I thought about people whose culture, upbringing and experiences were so very different from my own. It was a good thing to have done.

Chapter Ten

Maidenhead

I HAD not been at home more than three or four days when by chance I met John B, a school friend of my elder brother's. He was managing director of a quarrying firm, a subsidiary of a large engineering firm for whom he worked as a consultant. Learning that I was temporarily unemployed, he suggested I should go to Maidenhead to manage a plant which converted garbage and sewage sludge (more nicely described as habitation waste) into compost. I told him that my experience thus far had been on farms and I knew nothing of industrial processes. In other words I doubted my qualifications were good enough – besides which garbage and sewage sludge were not immediately attractive. Yet at the same time the idea of utilizing wastes for agricultural purposes – soil conditioning and enrichment – was something I had been interested in from my short time at the agricultural college where the relative virtues of organic manure – which mostly meant farmyard manure (FYM) – and artificial fertilizers – nitrogen, phosphate and potash (NPK) – were then being hotly debated.

One school of thought promoted the belief that all the feed a plant required to grow well was the right amounts of NPK plus perhaps a few trace elements, all of which could be got from a bag. Thus the term 'bagmuck' was coined.

The other school believed that because FYM was a natural product and it fitted into the tradition of mixed farming (livestock and arable crops), its use was more desirable. The final argument was – and is – that this system, which returns to the land what has been taken from it, had maintained fertility on farms for many generations, particularly since the advent of crop rotation systems. It was around this time that the Soil Association started and the pejorative phrase 'muck and magic' was coined.

In general I adhered to those beliefs. The arguments for and against went on for years and it is only relatively recently that both sides have given a little. The NPK school has lost the command it once enjoyed and has had to admit that there is more to a healthy fertile soil than a chemist can ensure.

I hesitated long enough to appear as if I were really thinking about it before agreeing to take the job, but only as a temporary appointment. John said he would see there was no bother over my exemption from military service and it was left that I would start three days later. As usual, I had not asked about salary, where I should live, how many men were employed or a score of other vital statistics.

During the war local authorities had to salvage paper and ferrous and non-ferrous metals separately for recycling. I don't recollect that anything else had to be saved by law but Maidenhead was excused this because the plant did the job. However, to make it pay many other kinds of stuff were saved: red rubber (not black), carpeting, bottles, broken glass (cullet), hessian bags (gunny to the trade), bones and dry batteries. In fact, anything which could be sold to make money. Not included were articles of silver. The men took all this material as part of their perks – and there was a lot of it – thousands of articles in one year which when sold perhaps more than made up for working in the dust from tipping garbage trucks, the smell of sewage and worst of all in hot weather the revolting stench from butchers' bones.

I had never regarded the contents of dustbins with much enthusiasm but I became quite amazed at the enormous variety of stuff people threw away and why. Why, for instance, should a Guards Officer's uniform, cleaned pressed and wrapped in tissue paper, or a half-hundredweight of perfectly edible New Zealand butter arrive in a dustcart? Had some black marketeer thrown it away when he feared detection? The butter was regarded with some suspicion but I tasted it and it seemed all right, and the men took it away, probably to sell to a café.

It never ceased to puzzle me as to the condition in which stuff was thrown away and I did a little research. Golden syrup tins, which the manufacturers wanted back, were always absolutely clean with not a trace of syrup left in their shiny insides, but potted meat jars, also wanted by the makers, were rarely clean. Somewhere in some dusty archive of a Public Cleansing Department there should still be an illuminating report I wrote on the subject. It showed that 80 per cent of all pots had some of the contents still remaining and over 10 per cent appeared to have been opened and discarded still full. Perhaps they went off in that particularly warm summer.

The trucks which collected the garbage from Maidenhead and district trundled into the plant, went up a steep ramp and tipped as near as possible to the edge of a twenty-foot-square iron screen. Four men stood on the screen and pulled and forked the rubbish over it. What fell through was mostly fine ash, small amounts of greenstuff and small bits of paper. This collected under the screen and was sold cheap to glasshouse growers for firing their boilers. The thermal value of the stuff warranted the cost of collection.

On the screen the men took out by hand anything and everything which was saleable. The rest was forked into the mouth of a powerful hammer mill which delivered it onto an endless belt with a magnetized pulley which took out the ferrous metals – including tin cans which got rolled into tight little balls – while the organic materials went on another endless conveyor to be deposited in the huge wooden pens or bays where the composting process started.

The pens were about forty foot long, fifteen foot wide and six foot high, and as the milled material fell from the conveyor belt two men forked it to make a yard-thick carpet and then built up the sides to make a giant dish. This completed, thousands of gallons of treated sewage sludge were pumped in until the dish was full. The sludge was about 98 per cent water which started to leach through the base and sides quite quickly and ran away back to the sewage works – and ultimately the Thames – leaving the solids trapped. More material was added on top and more sludge until it could absorb no more. Then it was mechanically shifted out onto a concrete pad, heaped and left for a few days to ferment, turned again and finally trucked off to maturing beds. Two months or so later it would be ready for sale to farmers and the many market gardens in the area now occupied by Heathrow Airport.

There was one exception to the sewage sludge. The Queen of Holland was living in exile in the district and the sewage from her establishment came to us untreated. That household must have been very primitive; the odour took me back to the privy at the bottom of the garden at Home Farm, but in this case there were no roses and honeysuckle growing to sweeten the surrounding air. When the lorry carrying the large cans came into the plant the men all held their noses and talked of a 'royal stink', which it certainly was.

The plant had been designed originally to utilize only garbage and sludge, but during the war the salvage side became increasingly important, especially of metals. But anything which could be saved and sold was collected. This was still the age of the dry battery and we sent scores of tons to London where what was useful to industry was removed – perhaps the carbon rods, I never knew. One good line was wine bottles. These were collected by a marine store dealer in Maidenhead and gently tipped into a heap. Beside the heap sat a man who all day and every day picked up one bottle at a time and holding it to his nose gave a long, analytical sniff. Then if he could detect nothing improper – paraffin was the commonest pollutant – he would put the bottle in an appropriate pile determined by colour – green, brown, amber or white, and size. Anything found wanting as to odour or integrity was hurled from him to the smashed heap of cullet. The pure ones went to wine bottlers, or so I assume.

I watched 'Sniffer' quite often. His upper lip and

nostrils were indelibly blackened and I wondered how after sniffing at a thousand bottles or more a day he could smell at all. I once asked him what he thought about as he picked, sniffed and stacked. 'You have to consecrate,' he said. 'Keep my mind on the job or an oil'd be bound to slip by.'

The plant machinery was all second-hand and break-downs were common. The main belt driving the hammer mill seemed to break every other day – but it didn't take long to repair. If the electric motor broke down it took ages to mend. In itself that didn't matter but while it was out of action the mountain of garbage got bigger and bigger and the bones grew smellier and smellier. It was an anxious business because we were contracted to take all the rubbish the council collected, so the pressure to get going and keep going was heavy.

Why no one was killed working in the plant must have been a matter of luck. At least three times while I was there packets of heavy ammunition went into the hammer mill where they made a frightful lot of noise but did no damage. Incendiary bombs were quite common. The men thought little of them and in fact used them to heat their kettle on an open brazier. They were difficult to ignite, but once going gave a ferocious heat. (This was before the days when incendiaries were also explosive.) It's strange that the men who collected the rubbish neither neglected to pick up nor rejected the potentially lethal objects before bringing them into the plant; for instance a sinister-looking hundred pound bomb. They can hardly have failed to notice that! Of course neither I nor anyone else knew whether it was dangerous or not, so holding my breath I hefted it onto the back seat of my Austin Mulliner saloon (with brass door handles, hooter button and advance and retard levers) and drove to Maidenhead police station. As I drew up outside – too sharply perhaps – the bomb rolled off the seat and onto the floor with a thud behind me. I didn't like that and the police didn't like it at all, and from a distance told me to drive it to a riverside meadow and leave it in the car to be looked after by the army. This I did and that the army did also, 'liberating' my spare wheel at the same time. I didn't blame them – the bomb disposal men were the bravest of the brave.

Much safer to handle was a stuffed grizzly bear, a curious animal eight foot tall, somewhat moth-eaten and lacking an eye. I imagined it must have come from the Bear Hotel in Maidenhead. The men tried standing it upright at the entrance to the yard where, until a careless garbage truck knocked it down, it enlivened the otherwise unremarkable landscape.

The hammer mill coped with bicycles, truckle beds, dustbins and a load of condemned oranges as well as the orange skins from a marmalade factory, but one thing it jibbed at was a dead sheep. Dogs and cats caused no trouble, but that sheep stopped the mill dead. The sheep's intestine is catgut and it was wound round so tight that it had to be cut from the hammers.

John B came down several times, partly to see how I was getting on and partly to introduce me to the electrically powered canoes which could be hired from Skindles Hotel on the Thames. These boats, shaped rather like Red Indian canoes, were very nearly silent – a faint purr would be a fair description of the noise they made. We went upstream beyond Boulters Lock to where in the distance we could just see Cliveden. Then back for a meal at Skindles, whose chefs hadn't heard there was a war on, or if they had, managed to ignore the fact. But generally there was very little time for pleasure.

Not every buyer was pleased. One man took fifty tons of compost before it was properly matured. He was in a hurry, but stacked it for a few days – it was a holiday time – and when he came to spread it the whole lot had spontaneously combusted. All he was left with among the ashes was the finely broken glass which could never be separated out in the plant. (Nor, had there been any, could we have separated the plastic film which is a bugbear of modern rubbish treatment plants.)

I'm not sure how beneficial in plant nutrient terms the compost was, as unfortunately, the trial plots which I set up on obliging growers' farms were not evaluated by the time I left. But since it contained a little of everything and a lot of some, it ought to have been good. It was not uniform at all times, as it varied according to season, the best time being when green-stuff was in abundance. It certainly did improve soil texture, making heavy land lighter and easier to work, and light land more retentive of moisture.

The Maidenhead plant was a pilot. As a result of its being written about and visited by sanitary engineers, similar plants were put up in several countries, New Zealand and India among them, but the idea never took off in Britain until recently.

It was always understood that the job was temporary. The time came when I had had enough of the dust and smell of bones and burning boots, which were more commonly used than incendiary bombs to boil the men's kettle, and longed for the fresher air of the country, and rather more interesting company than the men at the plant afforded, good men though they were. It's an odd fact but I have always found men working with garbage or sewage to be particularly cheerful – and healthy and easy to get on with. It is a great mistake to think that working with sewage is 'unhealthy'.

There was another and compelling reason for my wanting to leave Maidenhead. For some months I had whenever possible gone down for weekends to a pacifist community of mostly young people living in a large Edwardian house at Langham near Colchester, and I had fallen in love with Deirdre, a girl who was living there and who soon became my wife. (And remained so until her untimely death fifty-five years on.)

For the time being I was tied to Maidenhead. John B said I could leave once I had found someone to take on my job. It took time, but eventually I was free to go. By this time, however, the RAF had commandeered the house at Langham and the community had to find somewhere else to live. It was decided to buy a farm and work it communally and after a short search they found a very suitable three hundred acres with a large house and four cottages – enough to house as many as were likely to want an agricultural life. Deirdre was among them and when it was suggested and voted I should join them as farm manager, I agreed to throw in my lot.

In no way can I regret taking on that job. It taught me a lot about myself and how community living, so attractive in theory, can become very emotionally tangled and unhappy. Not least of my difficulties were basic things like persuading people to do certain jobs. For instance, horses had to be fed and groomed an hour

119

in advance of work starting, and that meant getting up an hour or more earlier than anyone else. Not fair, said the horsemen. Another vexation was that a few but vociferous members wanted to be paid the agricultural minimum. The argument was that to take less would mean they were blackleg labour. Fine, but since the farm had not started to earn, had no income, but plenty of debts, ordinary wages were impossible.

I knew, although I liked and admired many members of the community and the farm was a fine and productive one, that this was not my scene. Nor was Deirdre comfortable in this situation, so the decision to leave was easy: not so simple was where to go. This was decided for us when John B, hearing I was unemployed once again, called one evening.

Our conversation was brief. He told me his company had bought a farm in West Suffolk and he was looking for a manager to replace the existing one. Would I be interested in taking the job? I did not know what to say. I was being offered charge of seven hundred acres of heavy, very heavy clay land when all my limited experience had been on light and easily worked, free-draining soils. I told John B what he already knew – that I was not qualified. But he persisted and persuaded me that if I had a few weeks in the farm office, did the books and generally kept an eye on things, I would be ready to take over when the present occupant left. So with more than a few doubts about the wisdom of it, I agreed to take on the job. I didn't ask what the pay was, nor where we would live – mere details compared with major concerns such as the size of the farm: about twice the average for those days.

Chapter Eleven

Appleacre

DEIRDRE and I were married in the Newmarket Registry Office. Afterwards we swam in a place very like paradise on the banks of the River Stour. The sun was shining from a clear sky broken here and there by towers of brilliant white cumulus cloud. It was very, very hot, but a whisper of wind rustling the tall purple loosestrife, the sound of green rushes at the water's edge and the scent of bruised wild mint, sharp yet sweet, took the edge from the burning heat.

It was a wonderful time made even lovelier as we swam in the pale amber water. I had known that remote and private swimming place since childhood but never before enjoyed swimming as on that day. Swimming under water among the yellow water lilies, we took on a faint gold-washed colour; it was all beautiful.

The memory was romantic enough to keep us cheerful as we approached Appleacre Farm. Rose-coloured spectacles would have helped because at first sight it was not at all romantic. In fact, viewed from the Clare–Bury St Edmunds road, lacking trees and hedges, it looked lonely and featureless: only a shallow swale on the west side of the long stony drive relieved the monotony of the landscape. Further up the drive a few elms round the horse pond made it a little less desolate. On the east side were good brick stables and a fine bricked bullock yard which was roofed round the walls to allow the animals to feed in the dry. Alongside this was a brick and timber barn, much too small for a farm of seven hundred acres. Neither was the granary opposite with a steep wooden stair of any size. The rest of the buildings were of a more temporary nature: two very home-made looking Dutch barns, a piggery, fuel store and a cart lodge.

The house stood across the yard from the buildings. It was basically Elizabethan or earlier. Bits of it were alleged to be of Domesday Book date, and if the cellars were anything to go by, that may well have been the case. Like so many farmhouses it had a red-brick Georgian face slapped on the west with sash windows to match. The east side had been extended at some time but instead of continuing the Georgian theme someone had made it mock Tudor. The small garden, a few fruit trees and the stand of old elms made it look warmer than it ever was. Not for nothing is Hundon known as 'Cold Hundon'.

We placed the gypsy caravan we had bought at the far side of a permanent pasture under the lee of Appleacre Wood and three hundred yards from the house and yards. Our water supply was a land drain, and anything else we wanted had to be carried by hand from the yard where Deirdre kept her bicycle ready for shopping in Clare – downhill about three and a half miles and uphill the same distance. Hard work when loaded with paraffin, bread and everything else we needed, and harder still when she was pregnant.

We had hoped to be in the house after a few weeks,

but there were snags, and in the event we lived in the caravan for something like ten months. The winter was a hard one and although the caravan stove, a miniature coal range, warmed the place very quickly, it cooled off even faster and at night during a week of severe frosts, condensation froze our blanketed feet to the wall at one end and our hair at the other.

There were real compensations for this rugged existence. Being hard on the edge of the forty acre wood we saw a lot of natural life. It was quiet and we often had hares at the foot of the caravan steps. Red squirrels danced – or it sounded like it – on the roof. A tawny owl perched only a few feet from our window. Foxes were common. There was no noise apart from aircraft – no radio, no gramophone and to begin with no infant cries either. There was always something to see: a swarm of longtailed tits working the oak trees, or nuthatches and tree creepers always on the move. Despite having been country born and bred, there was always something we had never seen before. But then that is always true: keep still and silent and something will happen. We were especially lucky since there was no path nearby and once for five weeks Deirdre, who kept to the van and the woods, saw only a straggle of men going homeward across a distant field.

We enjoyed even the bad weather, and the cramped quarters did nothing to spoil it. Even bathing in an oval galvanized tub with a maximum two gallons of hot water heated in a pan on the range was fun, but difficult since one could only sit with knees up, or stand and splash.

I didn't lose touch with Maidenhead. Unfortunately every few weeks I had to go back there and, to use John

B's words, 'Straighten things out' – usually a simple matter of finding out what had been sold, to whom and to issue bills, which the then manager seemed to find difficult. In some ways it was a relief to leave the farm where, apart from keeping an eye on the books and creating a rational accounting system, my only worthwhile job was to get the entire farm surveyed and mapped field by field so that when the time came to drain we'd know what we were about.

It was the little cooking range which finally got us out of the caravan. A tremendous gale whipped up the fire, the chimney got red-hot where it was hidden behind a mirror and the roof caught fire. Deirdre was alone and poured and threw what water there was at it but to no avail. In minutes the entire roof was ablaze and there was just time to get the infant son and a few bits and pieces out before one of the men, having spotted the fire, brought a three-wheel horse-drawn water cart across the meadow and dowsed the flames. Oblivious of all this, I was in the farm office and got to the scene when only the frame and wheels remained. The heat had been so intense the mirrors – there were a lot of built-in mirrors – had melted. All the brass trimmings – door knobs, lamp brackets – melted too. End of a fine traditional travellers' van and our life therein.

The fire was certainly unfortunate but the timing was excellent. Deirdre and infant son went off to her parents in Bath and I went into digs in Hundon until the house was free. Deirdre returned with news that her parents were leaving their large house for a smaller one at Wotton-under-Edge, where there would be no room for all their furniture; we could have the surplus.

124

There were tons of it, far more than we needed, and enough much later on to part-furnish the houses of all our children as well.

It is a sad truth that once we were installed, furniture in place, oil cooking stove and lamps in working order, I had so much to do outside that I scarcely knew how Deirdre managed to run the place as the family grew from one to three in four years.

As to the farm, my remit was an open one. John B said, 'Farm as well as you can, record what is done, keep the accounts and if you want any help you've only to shout!' That was a totally unwarranted expression of faith in my capabilities but it had an invigorating effect on me, although I would rather have had firmer guidelines.

I had one advantage, I was not coming into the farm cold. During surveying I had for days on end acted as staff carrier and walked not only into every field, but all over them. So I already knew the land in fair detail: the corners difficult to get the plough to, the wet areas, and of course the hedges and ditches – all the basic things that have to be known in order to work any farm.

I wanted to get to know the men. Fourteen men had worked there for years and there were two boys not long from school. I had recruited a new foreman. Some of their names I've now forgotten but in my mind's eye I can see Walter and Bert Cook, stolid, quiet father and son; Ernie Missen, bright and dark and not long married; Jim Taylor, thin, sad, always made me think of a jockey who'd just lost a race, head horseman; Jack Murkin, a tall, handsome man, second horseman; Bill Betts who drove the tractor, a humorous chap who'd need to be, seeing the tractor was about as old as he was. The oldest man was Bob Missen, who kept the yard swept and clean and milked Janet, the house cow. Thatching was his real job. He had a game leg but that didn't stop him going up and down the thatching ladder.

The two brothers Jim and Bobby Thorogood and Horry Orbell complete the list. Horry should come last for he always was! A microcephalic whose head was no bigger than a coconut, he often got jobs none of the others wanted, but he was ever cheerful, never complained and took the mild ragging he came in for with a smile. Horry was not too well co-ordinated and was always tripping over fork or spade or whatever he was carrying. Coming into the yard from the fields at night, he would be yards behind everyone else, stumbling along, dropping his dinner bag or his tools, picking them up again, always losing the race. Cyril, the new foreman, a few years older than me, knew his job and had had more experience of heavy land than I. He was chapel and given to humming hymns or singing them, which was worse.

In one respect all these men (bar the foreman) were markedly different from the men I'd worked with in East Suffolk. They moved much more slowly and for good reason. This was heavy boulder clay country, and if for half the year and more you are walking about with half a stone of sticky wet clay on both boots, you get out of the habit of walking briskly even when unencumbered.

Initially I'm sure the men regarded me with a degree of suspicion. I was younger than all but three of them, I had no local background and odder still I had been living in a caravan, which is not a thing proper bosses do. It is hard to understand now, but the men obviously felt uncomfortable being talked to or asked their opinions about some aspect of work. It was awkward for me because they had detailed knowledge about the farm which I had yet to gain. They were an important source of information.

Why this difficulty? The fact is that for all their lives – and that of their forebears too – farm labourers were treated like serfs. They were bottom of the heap, and landowners and farmers would have them stay there. This was, I believe, especially true of that backward part of West Suffolk. In 1923 the farm workers went on strike. It quickly spread in a way farmers regarded as dangerous. Although in the end the workers got little or nothing of what they were demanding, the fact that they actually combined, spoke out and made their cause known made farmers apprehensive. Perhaps for the first time farmers realized they could be hurt by the men they employed, especially the stockmen. That was all a generation ago, but it was still remembered, and bad feelings engendered in both farmers and men persisted.

Only a few years before I came on the scene, the men at Appleacre had had to sign a form of contract in which one clause laid down that in the event of it being too wet, they could be sent home without pay. Of course not all farmers behaved so harshly to their men. There were many good, benevolent employers who treated their men as they should, but I think they were a minority in that part of Suffolk.

So it took time to get on easy terms with the men. Some I liked very much; Jack Murkin was one. He was ploughing on a hard, dry stubble one morning when I walked over to see how he was doing. Wanting to demonstrate my ploughing skill I asked him to make way for me. He stood aside, I took the plough handles and lines and gave the word to go. Within five seconds the point dug in, the handles flew up to my chin and the horses stopped dead.

Try again. I pulled the plough back, started the horses and did my best to keep the implement on an even keel. No good, It either skittered about on the surface, merely scratching the earth, or again dug itself in to a full stop. 'Jack,' I said, 'I'm making a fool of myself. I'm used to the Ransomes YL ploughs, the iron-wheeled ones. These wooden-beam things would take me some getting used to . . . Here you carry on.' Jack took the handles and grinning sideways remarked, 'We reckon anyone can plough with a wheeled plough – boy's tool. Anyway, they wouldn't be no good on this land – they're light land things.'

I felt suitably small as I watched him carry on effort-lessly balancing the implement to plough a perfect furrow. He was good. He was master of a craft to the point where it becomes an art. I never tried again – no time and no wish to look foolish. The thought comes to me that farmers, and I plead guilty myself, always say 'I ploughed', 'I drilled', 'I mucked' or 'I harrowed' and so on, when of course more often than not it is the men who do those things. Direction is needed, but the work is done by other hands.

I took over the farm in October. The ploughing was well advanced and most of the winter wheats were sown and up. Winter bean drilling had started, using a four-row drill rather than the now old-fashioned bean drill attachment. A box which was driven by a small land wheel dribbled the seed out in a reasonably regular flow to drop at the bottom of the furrow – so they were covered as the plough moved forward. To get the desired row spacing, the drill was turned on every second or third furrow. There's no doubt this method made for good even germination, but it was slow.

So far as the routine land work was concerned, I had little to worry about. The cropping was decided, fertilizers in store ready for use in the spring and everything running pretty smoothly. The weather was kind and we were able to get much out on to the field where in the spring we would grow roots.

The piggery was empty, or as good as, just a half-dozen left-overs from the last batch which hadn't achieved bacon weight. Rather than start breeding, although I would have liked to, I bought in a hundred eight-week-old blue and white weaners from Bury St Edmunds market.

Pigs, given the chance, are the cleanest animals on earth. They will always dung as far away from their bedding as they can and once the spot is chosen they keep to it. Pigs have to be fed twice a day and as a general rule mucked out once a week. In our piggery each of the pens had a door opening onto the central passage. The feed troughs were just to one side of the doors and it was easy to empty a bucket over the short wall into the troughs. That was fine, but quite properly the pigs dunged *away* from the feed troughs right at the back of the pens, so to muck out meant opening the door and forking the dung and wet straw into the passage which was too narrow to allow more than a handbarrow. (There should have been a long and wide passage at the back of the pens so that the muck could be forked straight into a tumbril; after two years this was fixed.) But for the time being a hundred pigs made more work than Bob Missen with his gammy leg could do on his own, so on mucking out days, usually Saturday mornings, the two boys, Bobby and Jim, were detailed to help.

Managing the cattle was simpler. The big double doors to the part-covered yard allowed room for the horse and tumbril to bring in feed and litter. This was also old Bob's job and I know he delighted as I did to see bullocks in deep clean straw. The old chap was always about the place. The sound of iron tumbril wheels, the rattle of pails and the shouts at the pigs to 'Come on outa there' or 'Git you in there' when all the other men were out in the fields made a background telling the place was alive.

Chapter Twelve

Settling In

THERE is a farming adage which I'd heard a hundred times: 'Look after the outside edges and the middle will look after itself.' It is a saying, hoary with age, which we like to trot out partly for its obvious truth and partly because it is agricultural gospel, tastes nice and needs no further explanation or discussion.

The three roadside fields were hedgeless and the ditches in decent order, but going further into the farm where it widened out (but could not be seen from the road!) less attention had been paid to 'the edges'. I did not want to do away with the hedges altogether, as has become fashionable, but these were taking up too much land. Some were fifteen foot wide and thorn, field maple and elm had grown as wide as they were high. Add dogwood and brambles and in time the hedges had spread to cover the banks (the Suffolk term is brews), making it impossible to get at the ditches.

This is how it happens. Gradually over the years, burrowing rabbits, rats and moles scrabble about moving earth from the banks to roll down to the moist ditch bottom where fallen leaves and bits of rotten wood make a fine bed for brambles to root in. Another year or two and not only have brambles' long arms rooted, but elm suckers, willow and a mass of small plants

131

become established, and soon the ditch is full and no longer capable of taking water away. Plants seeking light move ever outwards into the field.

On very heavy land tall hedges are a nuisance anyway. The land in the shade they cast dries out more slowly than in the middle of the field and this may slow up cultivations and certainly delays corn ripening. Too often at harvest time we had to leave wide uncut strips round the outside because the corn was still green.

Fourteen men may sound a lot, but to get round the miles of hedges and ditches using hand labour only – with all the ordinary work to do as well – would have taken years. I couldn't wait. Help was needed. During the time when I was a pupil in East Suffolk, I was woken one night by the thunderous roar of a machine. It came from a field the far side of a wood belonging to another farm. The noise was so extraordinary that the Guv'nor's son and I got up and walked through the wood to find out what was going on. It was a gyrotiller, the first and only one of two I have ever seen.

Originally designed and made for cultivating sugar cane land, they were at that time the largest and most powerful agricultural machines in the country. Their engines were so heavy that they had a small car petrol engine clagged on the side in order to turn over and start the main engine. If for no other reason than their sheer size, they created a sensation wherever they went.

One was working in north Essex and having seen what it could do I hired it. It couldn't cut a hedge or dig a ditch but it could crawl slowly along the field edges, tight to ditch banks, and with its massive contra-rotating, inter-meshing, claw-shaped tines, drag out brambles, elm suckers and even sizable young trees. The beat of its engine and the abrupt 'whump' when it got hold of something extra heavy could be heard for miles. Farmers and all sorts came to watch and wonder. It did exactly what I wanted. When the tangled mass of brambles and trees had been gathered and burned, we had gained many extra workable acres and a clear way to the remaining hedges and ditches.

Once it did more than required. It was crawling along a headland near the house when I heard it stop – and stay stopped. As it was hired by the hour, I wanted to know what was up. I found the driver had climbed down from his seat and was scratching his head looking at a hideous tangle of one and a half inch galvanized iron piping which it had dragged from the ground and knitted – there was no other word for it – round the tines' claws. On a different scale it was as if string had been fed into an egg beater. A proper mess: yards and yards of it. Worse still, it was our water supply!

The extraordinary thing was that although everyone knew our water came from a small concrete tower on the farm boundary, I had never wondered how the water got into it! In fact it had been automatically pumped from a neighbouring farm since the time when both farms were part of the same estate. Oddly enough, the supplier, our neighbour, was ignorant of it too.

No piped water in the house was hard on Deirdre. We installed a British Berkfeld Filter and got dubious-looking water from the pump in the cellar. I had never before seen a pump in a cellar, although a later house we lived in had a well there. As soon as possible we sank a deep bore – four hundred feet down into the chalk – and thereafter had unlimited supplies of water so hard it almost bruised you to bathe, and so rich in ferruginous bacteria it left towels stained dark Indian red. Water for the cattle and pigs was fetched from the pond where the horses drank.

I aimed to get as much hedging and ditching done in the first two years as possible because I realized that we'd be very unlikely to make a profit until the third – so I thought let's get the losses over quickly and there-after enjoy the profits. We needed more muscle, more strength. Casual labour had long since gone, the young ones into the armed forces, and the elderly and newly retired would not have been tough enough for the work. Then out of nowhere Michael and Patrick, two large, curly haired Irishmen walked into the yard. Had I work for them?

'Do you do any hedging – done any ditching at all?'

'Anyone would have to be older to have done more, sorr,' said Patrick, and Michael chimed in, 'We've just finished a sixty-two chain hedge and ditch for Mr Morton across the river at Pentlow. You ask him if we can ditch!' Not to be left out, Patrick added with emphasis, 'He'll tell you we'd make a grand job of any hedge or any ditch you like to show us.'

I said okay, we'll see how you get on and walked with them to look at the first bit I wanted doing. We did a bit of a haggle over the price but it was a terribly overgrown hedge and the ditch was more than level full with wet rubbish which none of our men would have relished tackling, so I didn't push too hard on price.

From that day onward for a year or more Michael and Patrick became part of the scenery. They looked after themselves, slept on straw-filled sacks in the granary, got drunk two nights a week and seemed none the worse for it in the mornings. Everyone bar the foreman, who had a thing about alcohol, enjoyed their company. They played merry hell with the local maidens and caused extra scandal by setting one of their beds on fire. I had banned smoking in the granary – but wasted my breath. Twice later they set their own beds afire while under the influence. Since they were sleeping over the fuel store with a tank of 1700 gallons of t.v.o. and fifty of petrol, it was just as well the Lord looks after drunkards as well as little children. Not that they were alcoholics. Weekdays they drank gallons of strong black tea. 'Have ye a pinch of tea, missus? Michael forgot to buy ut' was a regular call at the door. They seemed to live on vast quantities of bread, an occasional pan of boiled potatoes and cigarettes – not enough of a diet to sustain big, hard-working men. But it did.

It was alleged that from the time they left school to the age of twenty-one Irish boys didn't rush to find work. Rather they knocked about at home, went out with the lads for a bit of rabbiting or fishing and then at the end of this extended holiday made up for it by working like the devil. There is truth in it.

The first job they took on was this tallest and ugliest hedge on the farm. It had several thirty foot elms, masses of blackthorn, hawthorn, dogwood and so on with bramble and long arms of sharp-hooked dog rose running and tangling through everything. Patrick and Michael went at that job as if life depended on it. I have never seen men let loose so much fierce and sustained energy. There was a price to pay for this. Within three days two axe handles, one long-handled and one short-handled slasher, a billhook and a spade haft had been smashed. Later on I think they were more restrained, but my visits to the village smithy and the Clare ironmonger carrying an armful of broken tools were depressingly regular during the time they were with us.

Coming from west of Cork, they were wonderful talkers and their language full of imagery. 'There was this day, sorr, we were living in a sort of barn affair and Michael and me had a bit of a fight. Sure it wasn't over anything at all. He'd a drop taken and instead of fighting like a man, he picks up a lump of soap and flings it at my head. I dodged and no word of a lie, sorr, that soap went right straight through the wall behind me! I'd have had no head on me shoulders this day if it had hit me; God save us, he's a terrible strong feller he is so.' It must have been a hard block of yellow Monkey brand soap.

The Irishmen were less popular with our men than with me. They may have admired their muscle and their success with the girls, but they didn't anyway approve. As Ernie said, 'They go at it – they don't *pace* theirselves.' I could understand it was disturbing to see men not pacing, not, as it were, measuring their effort or 'taking it steady' as is our English custom.

The two Irish were not enough and I applied to the WarAg for additional labour and to my surprise – for my relations with that body were not harmonious – they responded by sending two German POWs: Heinrich, who quickly became Henry, and August, more difficult, was just Orgus. They were aged fifty or thereabouts – small farmers from neighbouring parishes not far from the Dutch border. They had been in some sort of local defence force for only two weeks when they were captured. We gave them a room and the back kitchen and they looked after themselves entirely. We supplemented their POW rations and they added to ours because after work if there was still light they set about the vegetable garden growing onions, lettuce and greenstuff.

We might have expected the men to actively dislike Henry and August, but it proved not so. In a very short time they were accepted, not only as good workers but as good men. There was a slight communication problem. My German was small and the men had none. On his part, Henry picked up quite a lot of English but at the end of the year or more he was with us, August had 'Good morning' and 'Water cart' and nothing else. If he had a rather limited vocabulary, he understood what was said to him so all was well.

Fieldwork in the first six months consisted of finishing the ploughing – getting the land set up to expose as great a furrow surface as possible for the frost to act on – and then as spring got nearer, cultivating with ducks-foot or very heavy crab harrows, leaving the final light harrows to give a good seed-bed tilth. Bill Betts did most of the ploughing and ducksfoot cultivating with the ancient International 10/20 tractor which he struggled with all winter. It was a brute of a machine. So was the Fordson. It was an industrial model with gear ratios unsuited to land work. Both were on iron spud wheels which broke up the surface of what little hard yard there was. I suppose there were tractors with rubber tyres somewhere about by then, but I never saw one until later.

It seemed to me that most of the first six months was spent preparing for what should happen next – and that is always true of farming: one eye on the now but always looking to the future: in this case when we could start draining in the following year.

There was plenty else to do. There were three stacks to thresh. Just why the old manager had left them, not for one, but two seasons, is a mystery. One was a linseed stack and the other two, which we tried first, were oats. Those stacks stood side by side with enough space between them to stand the threshing drum, so both could be threshed without having to move it. The foreman and Jim, the head horseman, told me they reckoned the stacks were so infested with vermin they'd prove a waste of time. Walter swore that if you walked between the stacks, they leaned away from you as the vermin moved over! Bert, his son, calculated aloud that the weight of the beasts would exceed the corn threshed. They were all proved too right.

The men on top of the stack who should have been forking sheaves down to the man feeding the drum found no sheaves. Their bonds had all been gnawed through by mice. I watched for ten minutes as the chaps threw the smelly straw and bits of oat-flight about and didn't need telling the exercise was useless and called it off. The foreman looked down his nose and reminded me of his prediction. What to do with the stacks? They were too near the buildings to set fire to and in the end I got Horry and the boys Bobby and Jim to pull them down – not a difficult job – and spread the mess about so the mice would leave. They – the mice, thousands of them, – did leave, but slowly, and for weeks the yard was hunted by kestrels, owls, cats, stoats, weasels and a pair of foxes. There were no rats. Rats and mice don't care for each other's company.

Having learned one lesson with the oats I had a more careful look at the linseed stack. It was in the corner – an unploughable corner – of a field well away from the yard. It had not been thatched and as I approached four small wild kittens peeped out from halfway up one side. I could see there was nothing to be gained by trying to thresh. It was a wet mess, and leaving it for a few weeks to allow the kittens to grow up, I set fire to it. It burned better than I thought it would: some of the oily seed had escaped the rodents.

When Michael and Patrick were at work – and that was most days – I'd walk over to have a look, often carrying a newly repaired tool. They'd give me the time of day but not stop swinging the axe, chopping or slashing through lesser stems unless it was to light cigarettes. They wanted money; that's why they worked so long and so hard. Patrick hoped, or so he said, to buy a small place of his own. Michael said nothing about his hopes but their weekend boozing must have made a hole in their savings. Perhaps this was one of their attractions. Whatever they did, work or play, they did with such vigour and gusto that one felt drawn to their enthusiasm.

They finished the long and worst hedge in under a month and started on the ditch. The amount of hard graft they got through was astonishing. They dug down to the original ditch bottom – not less than five foot below field level, cutting roots and flinging the spoil out into the field as far as they could. Then they'd give the bottom an even fall so when the water drained it, it would also flow out. Lastly they sloped and shaped and slapped the ditch sides with spades leaving them smooth. The newly exposed clay shone yellow and silky. If the drainers got their levels right, the water would get away from every part of the field.

That winter we only drained one field. It was not where Patrick and Michael had been working, but one nearer the road which already had a decent ditch. Put very simply, tile draining, which is the system we used, consisted of laying porous clay pipes below ground to carry water into a ditch.

It was not all that simple. First you had to find how the land slopes – and it may have been in more than

one direction. After deciding on the best layout for the drains, trenches were dug. We used to dig them by hand, but just before the war, machine diggers had become available and our contractor had one. So instead of men digging trenches nine inches wide and three foot deep into the clay, the machine marched steadily across the land leaving neat clean trenches ready to receive the tiles. My guess is that this machine reduced the labour required by 99 per cent, and we were grateful for it. I think the machine may have been American and was called a Buckeye. Anyway, it did a good job.

The trenches – much narrower than could be done by hand – were laid across rather than with the slope of the land, but always ensuring enough fall for water to flow. Next the tiles were laid in the bottom. We used standard three-inch diameter, foot-long tiles laid, with the aid of a long-handled tile hook, by hand. Butted up tight to each other they formed a continuous pipe usually taking water into a 'main' of larger diameter tiles (commonly four inch) laid with the fall of the land and thence to the ditch. This 'main' collected water from more than one line of tiles, thus increasing the volume of water and its capacity to keep the tiles from silting up.

A six-inch layer of coarse stone was laid on the tiles, the spoil from the trench on top of that and that part of the job was finished.

What remained was to mole drain. This was done by pulling a heavy steel blade with a 'mole' – a pointed steel cylinder at its base – just above the layer of stones and with the slope of the land. It could only be done using a very powerful tractor: ours wouldn't look at it.

The design of the drainage system for any field

depends on the nature of the soil – whether light and relatively free-draining, or heavy clay. 'Close' tiling where the lines could be as little as three yards apart was not so common and we generally dug trenches at eighteen yards or even wider intervals.

Few sights please more than to watch water pouring from a main drain into a ditch, knowing that the field will dry out that much faster and be easier to work and yield heavier crops in the future. The cost of draining was heavily subsidized. In theory each stage of tile draining operations was inspected by WarAg Officials. I don't recollect it happening, but we had of course to submit receipts for tiles, stone and contractors' work before getting the subsidy.

The government was out-of-the-ordinary wise in subsidizing draining, hedging and ditching and liming. These gave quite quick returns in terms of extra food grown, but also laid the foundations for long-term land improvement. Appleacre didn't need lime – boulder clay usually has a proportion of chalk in it – but I was after any and all the subsidies going for things we needed.

Deirdre cooked on a three-burner oil stove; it was a Florence, which once mastered worked wonderfully well. It gave the whole house a faint paraffiny smell. We had several sorts of oil lamp. The duplex had a double wick and an oval chimney and was easy to light and use. More difficult to manage, but giving a whiter and brighter light, were the Aladdins. They had mantles like gas mantles which, unless the wicks were kept clean and not turned up too fast or far, sooted up, sending huge oily smuts floating in the air to settle over everything. The stink this made was horrible. The third – we had only one of them – was a paraffin-burning pressure lamp which had to be pre-heated with methylated spirit and then pumped up as hard as was prudent. It gave a terrific light but was very like a bomb. Twice it got knocked and fell from its hook and both times it went out to spray paraffin over our supper. We were very lucky.

'Have you done the lamps?' was a daily question. It was, I am slightly ashamed to say, one of the few domestic chores which fell to me. Deirdre disliked getting paraffin oil on her hands – difficult to get off and liable to taint whatever she was cooking. It happened only very rarely, but, as anyone who used paraffin will tell you, sooner or later it is bound to happen.

I still like the smell where paraffin lamps and heaters are used, especially when it is combined with the faint odour of damp, found nowadays but rarely, and then most likely in little-used village churches. It takes me back in a flash to home, childhood and the later farms we lived in.

We didn't feel it a hardship to be without electricity. Few farms and fewer village houses had it. We just didn't think about it at all. Our hot water supply came from a large, hungry, black-leaded boiler in the old kitchen which we gave over to Henry and August. They looked after it, while Deirdre had her kitchen and oil stove nearer the school room where we ate. It may have been a school room at one time but nobody knew when. It had an eight-foot-long table with ancient ink stains sunk deep into the wood, a massive piece of furniture which must have been built in situ. We had to take it to pieces when we left the farm, and it is still in the family. There was a wash-up and scullery sort of

143

room, very cold but looking out across the yard to the horse pond where moorhens and ducks swam under the shade of the tall elms. Washing up was a job nobody wanted. The water was so hard even the finest soap-flakes failed to work: they broke up but wouldn't dissolve. Plates and dishes gradually accumulated a slightly greasy patina which could only be removed by generous treatments of soda in hot water. I suppose most of my generation will remember scraping and scratching mutton fat from dinner plates and at the same time give thanks for modern detergents which make washing up a positive pleasure.

We could have done with a bit more heat. On some mornings the windows in the bathroom and scullery were thick with wonderful frost flowers in patterns as thick and rich as the most sumptuous Victorian furnishings. All they lacked was colour. As the rooms got warm, the flowers and ferns melted and dripped to the sills and thence to the floors, which may have been the reason for signs of rot in the floorboards under the windows.

For the first four years Deirdre had no help in the house and apart from a few words about bringing mud in on my boots − a few words quite often repeated − she kept any complaints she had to herself. There was plenty to keep her occupied, for on top of cleaning, cooking and looking after the first, second and third infants and me, she gardened and made jams and marmalade and butter and cheese. We were very lucky that the house cow happened to be a Jersey-Friesian cross which gave milk in Friesian quantities and Jersey quality; in other words a great deal of extremely rich milk.

Deirdre made butter in an old-fashioned wooden

end-over-end churn, which, depending on the temperature of the weather and the cream, 'came' slowly or quickly. Sometimes it seemed she turned that handle for hours until the sound in the churn changed from an even sort of swishy slop to an irregular flop, flop, flop. The butter milk was drained off to be used in pancakes. Several changes of cold salt water went into the churn with the butter until the last traces of butter milk had gone and the butter itself was firm. After that the water was squeezed out by hand in the keeler and all that was left to do was to smack it into shape – pats or rounds – with wooden butter hands, a most satisfying job.

The cream the butter was made from was skimmed from milk left overnight in wide shallow pans. This left the skim (flet) milk which Deirdre tried making into flet cheese. It was quite simple. The skim milk was put in a large bowl, and rennet and salt added and the mixture left to work. Then it was cut or crumbled to release the water, put in a muslin bag to hang, drip and harden. There's no doubt it was highly nutritious but it lived up to Robert Bloomfield's description in *The Farmer's Boy*:

> '. . . in the hog-trough rests in perfect spite,
> Too big to swallow, and too hard to bite.'

By modern standards I would be considered an unsatisfactory paterfamilias. I only once ever pushed a pram. Actually I didn't push: I *pulled* it out of the deep mud where it was stuck. Deirdre was stuck too. But I did once or twice change a nappy and even washed them as well. They were Harrington squares plus some thicker ones of terry towelling. Long years after the last child came out of nappies, we still used two old Harringtons every year for straining blackberry and apple or blackcurrant or damson juice ready to make into jelly. The fine muslin has taken on a delicate purple colour, and they look good for many years yet.

Chapter Thirteen

The Farming Seasons

'IN the Spring a young man's fancy lightly turns to thoughts of love.' So they may, but farmers on heavy land have other preoccupations. There is no time in the whole year when so much depends on their judgement to carry out the sequence of cultivations which will ensure a good start for the crops to be sown. Every day in the critical early days of March I walked the fields kicking the clods. Only by walking and feeling how the clods broke could I judge if the land were fit for drilling or needed more cultivation, whether to cultivate again, or hope to achieve the right tilth with crab and light harrows. The old chaps used to say that if the clods will pass between the drill coulters, that's enough for winter wheat. But for spring sown crops you need a fine tilth – an 'onion seed' bed. In other words, as fine a tilth as possible.

Everything turned on the weather. Given a strong wind and sun, the newly moved soil would quickly 'hazel' – growing lighter as the moisture was driven off. But let it rain and the onion bed, got by luck or labour or both, would turn into a porridge which must be worked over again to dry before drilling.

There was an old saying that unless you can sit bare-arsed on the soil without feeling a chill, it is not fit to drill barley. In the interests of science I tried this out in a secluded corner of a remote field and concluded it would never be fit to drill.

For the first few years I grew Spratt Archer and Plumage Archer barleys, later experimenting with Golden Archer as well, but I finished up growing only Spratt Archer, a variety most likely to make a sample wanted by the maltsters and to fetch the best prices. Other than barley the only spring cereals I tried were a small acreage of April Bearded wheat, an awned variety, and a field of naked oats (*Avena nu*). Neither were good yielders and I can't think now why I ever grew them.

Mangolds were becoming an old-fashioned crop but I grew them for the bullocks: I favoured Gatepost, a variety with a cylindrical root a foot and more deep. I reckon we got thirty tons an acre. Some say mangolds are an expensive way of carrying water to the stock-yard. True, the mangold does hold a lot of water, but in the form of sweet juice which cattle relish – it helps dry winter fodder to slip down.

Root crops – beet, mangolds, swedes and potatoes – are all labour-intensive, a term not invented at that time. The beet and mangolds came up as they say, 'thick as hairs on a cat's back' and had to be singled by hand. We couldn't afford the time on these jobs and I kept the acreage as low as was consistent with the demands of a rotation.

Peas did well: Harrisons Glory for harvesting dry, and tic beans and horse beans which we fed to pigs and cattle. Of 'small seeds' we grew red clovers: cowgrass or single-cut for feeding as stover (pronounced stuvver) to horses and cattle, and double-cut, where we took a light stover cut, followed after flowering by a seed cut.

148

(This was well suited to heavy land.) Then white clover, sainfoin, trefoil and lucerne: the lucerne for hay and the rest for seed. They were all undersown on spring barley using a Smyth Non Pareil drill. These drills, from Peasenhall, Suffolk, were virtually hand made and I doubt if the design had changed much in more than half a century. Made of wood and horse-drawn, they had a cup feed that distributed seed remarkably evenly. I don't doubt that on some small Suffolk farm there is still one in use.

We did drill some cereals with a metal drill which applied fertilizer at the same time. It was difficult to clean and when wet it corroded overnight. I paid twenty pounds for it second-hand.

The farm was grossly under-equipped and machinery hard to come by. The WarAg controlled allocations for almost all farm machines and I was forever filling application forms for a tractor, a crawler tractor, a combine harvester, not to mention simpler implements such as harrows or heavy Cambridge rolls. It was one thing to apply and another to get what you wanted, and it did not seem to depend much on the degree or urgency of need either. It worked best (I was told) if one knew someone influential on the Executive Committee, a body drawn mainly from the larger and long-established farmers in the county.

I was infuriated to see farmers already with tractors enough taking delivery of new ones while I battered on the WarAg doors in vain. East Suffolk's WarAg had a reputation for equitable dealing, West Suffolk's did not. One example of this was the case of the Newmarket Gallops. Not a single acre of this huge area ever came under the plough. No matter how short of food the country might be, this was sacred turf. It was clear the Jockey Club had more influence over events than the Ministry of Agriculture or the WarAg. East Suffolk regarded this as a national scandal – which it was. Being a newcomer I had no useful contacts in high places and it seemed that if I got on an allocation list my name would be at the bottom of it. I heard that it paid to offer a day or two of shooting to the right people. It was quite astonishing how many influential farmers spent several days a week knocking down game birds on other people's land.

'When June is come, then all the day I'll sit with my love in the scented hay,' sang Robert Bridges, who like many poets and novelists viewed haymaking a most romantic business. In times past when damsels in pretty bonnets raked and turned the new-mown grass it probably was. Certainly the scent would have been as sweet as or sweeter than it is today, but it was all hard labour which I suspect writers viewed from a distance. At

150

haysel my eye was fixed on the weather rather than love in the sweet-scented hay – for that's what I hoped it would turn out to be.

We grew short-term ryegrass-clover mixtures, and we started haymaking in mid-June. The sun shone, the wind blew, and the crop, not overheavy, dried quickly. We had cut the grass with a horse mower adapted for tractor draught. (We were constantly adapting and bodging implements for tractor use.) But once the grass was cut, all swathe turning, raking and carting to the stackyard was done with horses in the first year. In most years the hay would have been put into cocks to dry out but I reckoned this time it would not be necessary, so Jack Murkin laid out a thick bottom of wheat straw for a large stack and up it went.

That stack alone would not be enough to keep the horses and the bullocks I planned to fatten, but there was clover and stover yet to cut, and having undersown thirty acres of barley with ley mixtures, we'd be better placed in the coming years. On the whole I was feeling pleased with myself, a feeling which grew when, as soon as the stack was finished, we had two days of rain. What superb judgement!

Five days later my balloon of self-satisfaction was pricked. I got up as usual and walked across to the stables where Jim Taylor had been feeding and grooming for an hour or more. 'I reckon you orter have a look at the haystack. When I got the horses in I thought that'd got a bit of a nose on it.'

The stack was in the corner of the meadow nearest to the yard. I walked to it. He was right. I could see and smell steam gently rising from the roof into the cool morning air. Jim joined me. 'Getting warm, I reckon. I

151

did say I thought you was a bit sharp getting it in.'
Quite true, and kind of him to remind me.

Now a few degrees, a modest heat, the result of fermentation in the stack, is normal and acceptable, but if fermentation continues, it will get hotter and hotter until in the worst case it self-combusts – catch fire and be lost. I hoped it wasn't as bad as that, but how bad had to be determined. I fetched the stack iron, a six foot long and half-inch thick iron rod with a handle at one

end and a shallow hook at the other. I thrust it at breast height full length into the stack and left it for ten minutes before pulling it out. Everything depended on what the wisp of hay caught in the hook from the middle of the stack looked like. Well, the wisp was brown and moist and the iron too hot to hold. My reputation, for what it was worth, was dented, but the stack could yet be saved.

The outbreak of fire was not imminent, but the longer the stack was left the worse it would be. Speedy action was called for. The stack had to be turned. By eight o'clock we had a new stack bottom laid out: faggots first, the straw on top, and the elevator in position. Before starting, I made an open tunnel by leaning hurdles together in the shape of a tent from the outside edges across the whole length through which air could freely flow. This done, two men started forking the hot hay onto the elevator whence it fell to the new bottom. Each forkful was lightly fluffed in the process so that by

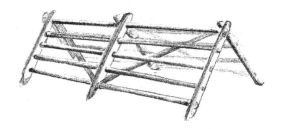

the time it was on the stack it was somewhat cooler and drier. It was a slow and tedious job.

As the stack was lowered to eaves level the hay was hotter and the men uncomfortable. 'My blinken feets are boiling. You could cook taters up here,' complained Ernie. So we stopped from time to time for them to cool off. Besides that, there was some danger of being overcome by the fermentation fumes.

Directly hay on the new stack covered the hurdle tunnel, I filled two corn sacks tightly packed with straw, which as the stack grew were pulled upwards. These left two vertical airways so now wind and air could get into the horizontal tunnel and up through the two 'chimneys'. As an added precaution I sprinkled rock salt on the stack at one-foot intervals to further inhibit fermentation. It worked. Fermentation slowed and then stopped and in due time the 'new' hay, slightly brown and sweet smelling, was eaten by horses and cattle with relish. I was pleased and relieved because I had never actually seen a stack treated that way and, strangely, neither had the men – that is, they knew about turning, but the use of airways was novel. I told no one I'd got the idea from a book.

The weeks between haysel and harvest are usually the easiest in the year; the farmer's holiday choice. Hoeing roots was the main work and doesn't call for much supervision. We horse-hoed sugar beet and mangolds partly to kill weeds and partly because we believed moving the top surface encouraged moisture and air to circulate and increase root growth. (That belief must have taken a knock, for today, hoeing roots is a memory belonging to the distant past and mourned by few. The chemists have won.)

I took no holidays. There was no petrol with which to get to the coast, which in any case was barb wired and mined, so we took the odd afternoon and picnicked in the woods with the children, or went to the Stour with them to swim. I'd have felt bad about taking any prolonged time off because I was already away from the farm at Maidenhead too often. So I was thankful Cyril the foreman was good at his job and I could go away knowing that everything would tick over all right. He was reliable and it's a pity that outside the farm we had nothing in common.

Harvest that year was nothing special, but the weather was kind and we had plenty of time to cut, trave, cart and stack, which is all that mattered. For that first harvest we had only two old horse binders. One we adapted for towing by tractor, the other we left as horse drawn. These binders were powered by the heavy bull wheel which took the whole weight of the machine. They made hard work for horses and if the ground were wet the wheel could skid instead of turn and stop the whole operation.

Setting up the sheaves was called shocking. In the bit of Essex where I was a pupil, it was called traving. In other parts of the country the common term was stooking, but wherever it was it was all hand work. The aim is to stand the leaning sheaves towards each other in an A to keep the ears from the ground. At Home Farm I was told to 'Shove the arse end hard to the ground and clap their ears together.' A well-made shock of three, four or five sheaves a side will shed rain for some time – but not for long! Depending on the weight of crop, one man would expect to set up six acres a day. It was hot work and murder if the crop had thistles. Horny hands we may have had, but shocking a good crop of wheat embellished with thistles left fingers scratched and bleeding, particularly at the base of the nails when fingers went between the sheaves and the hard twine which bound them together.

Once the fields were ready, we started to cart and stack. What was wanted was a double row of stacks, ideally each one of a size to take one day to thresh. Once one was finished, the opposite one could be threshed without moving the drum and straw pitcher, or the baler. In this way two corn stacks when threshed made one large straw stack, so in time we had one line of straw stacks in the space between where the corn stacks had been. At Home Farm the corn stacks were always boat ended – rather like a church nave but with an apse at both ends. At Appleacre stacks were right-angled, the roofs a simple gable – much the easiest to thatch. Nine by five yards was about the size for ten acres of an average crop.

Ten by six yards was favoured for a heavy crop of horse beans and just once we made a whopper – eleven by seven. Why such a monster I can't think, but I shall not forget the four days broken by rain that it took to thresh. The men carried the tilt up and down the long ladder many times – and a heavy cotton stack cloth

155

weighs! At the end of that harvest we had twenty-three corn stacks under the lea of Appleacre Wood, which gave more thatching than old Bob could manage alone so I got a travelling thatcher to help out. A well-built

stack, especially of wheat, will shed rain for a while, whereas barley, whose straw is more absorbent, soaks it up. But nothing is safe until it has a hat on. Many, many times the sound of rain on the bedroom windows fetched me out of deepest sleep. The men too. Jim, whom I saw first every morning, would put his head out of the chaffhouse door and cheer me up, 'I wook up at two and that were a proper downpour. I doubt the barley'll be sodden. More comen too by the look on it.' So helpful!

After the corn was all in we had the clovers to deal with. I opted, as most do, to thresh the red clover in the field. This meant getting in a contractor with a clover huller, a thresher specifically designed to deal with tiny seeds. Clover hulling in unquestionably the dirtiest and most choking job on the farm. On a still day the machine and men would be hidden in a heavy black cloud. Nobody wore masks although some put a hand-kerchief over their noses. To work all day long in this dense fog was hell.

Red clover is fertilized by bumble bees. This admir-able insect has enemies – the field mouse, and I believe the bank vole too, go down into the bees' nests in the hedge banks to eat the inhabitants or rob them of their larvae. Now one of the mouse's most active predators is the common cat, so a good number of half-wild cats about the place will help to ensure a good yield of seed . . . and fewer pheasant chicks.

Red clover seed is beautiful. Hard, heavy and shiny, the best – that is, the sample making most money – is reddish purple, and the more purple the better. We grew samples it was a pleasure to take to Bury St Edmunds market. It may have been luck, but I never remember making less than top price. We were still putting seed into combe sacks, which then weighed twenty stone. Few volunteers to carry them up the granary stair. I never did: I couldn't have. One of the oddities of marketing was that merchants bought red clover seed by the bushel and sold it by the pound for sowing. A little clover seed goes a long way – fourteen to twenty pounds an acre was enough.

Yields varied. In a bad year it might be less than one hundredweight an acre, but in one very good year, and it only happened once, we threshed out thirty-five hundredweight from ten acres. To give the arithmetic, that is 3,920 pounds weight or 56 bushels. The price, if my memory serves me well, was about £9 a bushel. Call it better than £50 an acre. That was real money and I returned from Bury smiling.

Even before harvest was finished, the tile drainers were at work on the stubbles so we could plough, cultivate and get as much winter wheat as possible in early and before the winter rain set in. Naturally the rain often got there first and I never quite got in the acreage I planned for. Always impatient, I wanted to drill in September, which most farmers at that time thought silly because it would make for 'winter proud' growth. In practice a lush growth didn't matter anyway. Older and more traditional men sometimes turned sheep in to graze the luxuriant 'winter proud' growth. I never did: hadn't any sheep anyway.

That winter I drilled two varieties of wheat: Square Heads Master and White Victor. By the standards of the time they both yielded reasonably well – twelve to fourteen combes an acre, sometimes a fraction more, making around one and a half tons. We *heard* of farmers growing two tons but didn't believe it. Today you wouldn't speak of your wheat yield unless it was four tons and more.

Every season has its special pleasures and walking bare stubble fields after harvest is one. The crisp crackly sound of boots tramping the sharp straw and the sudden whirr of wings as coveys of partridges streak away low over the ground, rise over the distant hedge and glide out of sight were somehow cheering. Partridges don't care for heavy land and over our six hundred acres of arable I reckon we rarely had more than ten or twelve coveys.

Having for so long been restricted by tall corn, the dogs went wild in the sudden freedom of open fields.

Even if the sharp stubble hurt their feet, they raced after hares and rabbits with the greatest joy. We'd a short-legged mongrel terrier which was forever hopeful of running down rabbits. She would streak off at top speed, never getting near her prey, and only giving up when exhausted. Seeing a vain chase from the top of the stack he was thatching, old Bob said, 'She want to find one with three legs! She lose her breath "prapsing" like she do.' I asked him what 'prapsing' might be. 'Do you hark at har. She's all the time yelling "praps I shall, praps I shan't", and see she puff herself out.' Prapsing was narrowly local and perfectly descriptive of the row an enthusiastic terrier makes in a hopeless chase.

We threshed several fields of wheat in the field which saved stacking. The grain was taken off the back of the drum into combe sacks and carted to the barn. Ordinarily two men would lift the sacks into the tumbril, but August, who was doing the carting, hefted the sacks up by himself. A combe of wheat weighs 18 stone: he treated them as if they were mere hundredweights. The Germans thought I was mad to stop harvest work at eight o'clock in the evening and noon on Saturdays while there was still light and the corn was dry.

I pestered the WarAg all year for a new and more powerful tractor or tractors than the elderly International 10/20 and Fordson, but with no luck. Since there was no hope of getting over the acres I wanted ploughed that autumn with those antiques and the horses, I got a steam plough contractor in. Steam ploughing was old-fashioned even then, but it was the answer to my prayers. The outfit consisted of two powerful steam engines, each with a horizontally slung winch under their bellies. One at each end of the field pulled the five-furrow balanced plough on some eight hundred yards of steel rope. One pulled, the other passive, then as the plough came up to the active engine, both moved up the headland and the passive engine became the active one. The plough, with one set of furrows cocked up behind (they were lowered and were in the earth on the reverse journey) went at tremendous speed, and quietly. The rushing sound of the turning soil and the whistle warning the engine driver at the other end that the plough had stopped was all. A man mounted on the plough was able to steer it round gentle curves. Childish perhaps, but I always rode for a few bouts. A most enjoyable sensation as the plough rushed along, like sailing with a following wind.

One advantage of steam ploughing was that there were no heavy tractor wheels panning the soil. (At that time and certainly when I was at the East Anglian Institute of Agriculture, there was serious discussion whether horses or tractors most panned the soil.) The disadvantage was the quantity of coal and water that steamers consumed. Working a distant field kept one man busy carting all day. The engines ploughed around fifteen acres a day.

We had two Suffolk colts bred on the farm and coming up to two years old. Jim, the head horseman, had bitted them – got them used to bridle and bit, and then a collar. That done, he hung chains on the collar attached to a heavy five-foot-long tree trunk, and drove the colt forward. The colt didn't like this at all and stood still. So Jim applied the whip; the colt rushed forward, whereupon Jim put his whole weight on the lines, pulling on the heavy bit so hard that the colt began to back toward the log. A slash of the whip and the animal rushed off again, was pulled back and so on and so on, repeated until it had learned what was expected of it. I told Jim he was needlessly violent, but he gave the stock answer, 'Ya gotta larn 'em who's master do they on't never be no good.'

Compared with some others Jim was gentle. A friend of mine in Lincolnshire watched a colt tied to a post by a ten foot line in the middle of a big dunghill. The horse was then thrashed and thrashed until its mouth was bleeding and, finally worn out trying to escape the lash, stood trembling and ready to flounder. That was bloody cruel. But my friend assured me that the horseman loved his horses and by the time they were ready to work they were quietly obedient and showed no fear of their master. I do not think that is sufficient excuse for such a method.

Before Jim started on the second colt I was awoken early one Sunday morning by the clop clop sound of horse hoofs in the yard. I went to the window thinking it had got out of the meadow, and if one was out, the rest would follow. I was astonished to see August *riding* the unbroken colt across the yard and disappearing behind the Dutch barn, only to reappear a few moments later riding toward the meadow where the other horses were grazing.

When Jim learned how the colt was gentled, he complained loudly, 'What do he know about breaking hosses? You'll see when that go to work there'll be trouble . . . and you'll know who to blame . . . that ain't right.' He never stopped moaning. After all, breaking youngsters was his job – and there was a head horseman's ten quid perks at the end. I gave him the money even if his job had been done for him. Neither of the colts was any trouble at work, so if there is a moral here it must be that some people can break horses without recourse to cruelty.

What was acceptable treatment of animals then, is no longer. For a very short time we had an old vet whose first act on going into the stable to look at a horse he'd never seen before was to give it a hefty blow on the nose with his fist. In answer to my question, he gave the same answer as Jim had, 'You gotta show 'em who's the master and they can't play up with you.' He never set foot on the farm again. To be fair, he was the last unqualified vet with a licence to practice. He was a very old and bad relic from the 'horse doctor' era.

I am not unduly sensitive but it is hard to imagine how farmers and drovers can watch impassively while cattle are driven with heavy blows about the markets, blows on their delicate snouts and tails twisted until you hear the ligaments snap. I once talked to the Bury auctioneer about it and he said 'I've got just so long to get a hundred and more cattle through the ring and if the drovers were gentlemen I'd never get done in a day. Anyway, they don't feel pain like we do!' Really?

Walking the farm, I usually carried a gun. We had to kill rabbits. They were too many and too hungry, eating the equivalent of at least ten acres of cereals a year. Fortunately, rabbits, like offal, were not rationed and they made a shilling or two a head. On Home Farm before the war, 'harvest' rabbits often couldn't be given away. I well remember burying eighty we'd shot out of one harvest field. It was different now. If it could be eaten, it was saleable!

Pigeons were a year-round target. They wrecked the peas in spring and when the snow covered their favourite

162

food – clover – they settled on kale, eating out the centres and making it useless for feed or seed. When the snow was exceptionally thick I put a white sheet over my shoulders and, standing in a ditch, shot the birds as they flew in. During weeks of hard frost and snow it was a waste of time and shot: they starved to death anyway.

I sold pigeons and rabbits to local butchers until I learned a Smithfield merchant paid much better. He said he would take rabbits, hares, pigeons and young rooks. Now Appleacre was justly famed for the numbers of rooks and jackdaws winter-roosting in the wood. The wood was divided by wide rides into four ten-acre squares and rooks roosted only in one quarter.

As the winter sun began to get low in the western sky, rooks started to fly in, not to the wood but to a field, not always the same one, a quarter of a mile or so away. They came first in pairs, then dozens and scores and hundreds until they covered ten acres as if it had been tarred solid black.

The rooks cawed and the jackdaws yacked for five or ten minutes while the last stragglers flew in. They were behaving very like a theatre audience waiting for the curtain to rise. Lots of chatter, sudden movements as if someone had disturbed the seating, and then as if by common consent all sound and movement ceased. Absolute silence, literally not a sound. Then out of this silence came a single voice: a series of measured, deep-toned caws from one, and I'm sure wise, old rook.

Who could say what the message was? A sermon, a word of warning about dangerous feeding grounds, a passage of corvine history for the youth? Whatever it was, it sounded grave and portentous. The address finished – it lasted only a minute or so – and the congregation chattered again until, again as if by common consent, they rose as a cloud and sailed into the wood. There the noise was deafening as they bickered and squabbled over perch space. The row went on until dark and was so loud it could be heard two miles away.

The ash trees in their chosen quarter were tall and young and were gradually being denuded of their smaller branches, broken off by the sheer weight of the birds. The ground underneath was covered with droppings smelling unpleasantly fishy. Experienced ornithologists estimated the roost as holding between ten and a hundred thousand birds! As Horry remarked 'There's hell an' all on 'em!' I reckon he was right.

Pigeons roosted in the wood too, although not near the rooks. I shot them for the pot because Deirdre had discovered the secrets of making pigeon pie. (There is a superstition that if you eat pigeon every day you'll become incurably bound. We ate a tidy few but never tested it to the limit.) After sending two hampers of pigeons to Smithfield I added rooks; during one winter I sent off hundreds and hundreds of rooks and pigeons packed together in their feathers. What they must have smelled like by the time they arrived in London I cannot imagine. I telephoned the merchant and asked where the birds went to. He answered briefly – for game pie in hotels and restaurants.

Chapter Fourteen

Buying and Selling

DURING the winter months I drove to Bury market
in the Willys Jeep at least once a fortnight. If I
were buying cattle I'd go in the morning but usually it
was afternoon when I headed for the Corn Hall. This
is among the most imposing buildings in Bury St
Edmunds with a main door flanked by tall pillars
supporting the entablature upon which are deeply
engraved the pious words THE EARTH IS THE LORD'S
AND THE FULNESS THEREOF, to which I would like
to have added, 'But only after the merchants have had
their cut.' Inside on a busy day there was a subdued
babel of voices as the merchants standing at their desks
– I suppose there must have been fifty of them – did
business with farmers and with each other. The seeds-
men such as Harold Sadd or Kings of Coggeshall
concentrated on clovers, grasses and other small seeds –
perhaps peas as well – but barley was the big thing. It
was said that more barley was bought and sold in Bury
than any other market in England.

I took my samples of barley in small cotton bags and
probably went to a merchant with whom I had never
dealt. I'd hand him the sample bag and he'd look at it.
He'd sniff at a poor thin sample and offer a price on the
spot, a low one, of course. This gave me some idea of

the market on that day. I might decide to sell there and then, but more likely I'd go to someone with whom I had previously had satisfactory dealings. This one might offer a higher price and the deal would be struck.

But if I were offering a malting sample, that is, a potentially more valuable barley which would be sold on by the merchant to a maltster, the procedure was longer. First he would have a look at the grain in the bag. He was looking for plump, thin-skinned, even-sized clean grain without signs of having been damp. That hurdle over, he would shake a portion of grain into a barley cutter. This was a hand-held instrument in two parts. The bottom bit had a hundred holes and the top bit was a sharp cutting blade. The merchant poured enough grain to fill the holes and then closed it, cutting each grain in half. Upon the opening of the instrument the interior of each grain was exposed, and bargaining began. The price depended upon how white and chalky the exposed surfaces of the grains were. If they were white all over − 100 per cent − fine. But should some grains look steely or flinty, then there'd be a lot of hum-ing and ha-ing before either a price was agreed or I'd take the sample to try my luck with other merchants. I had got some advance idea of the quality from rubbing out the grain from several ears in the field and biting them in half. Farmers still do today, although chemical analysis has, as with so many other aspects of grain selling, become the final arbiter.

With three or four different samples to show several merchants, it took an hour or more, and by the time I had done, the whole of the market floor would be covered with the half-grains discarded from the cutters. On the whole one traded with merchants who over a period had given decently fair prices, but there had to be a degree of mutual trust. The buyer had to be sure that the bulk would prove 'up to sample': it is not all that easy to determine the value of say a hundred quarters – that is seventeen and a half tons – from a half-pound sample.

An afternoon in the corn market could be valuable even if I were neither selling nor buying. There were the gossip and overheard remarks – 'Sadds are looking for Wild White seed'; 'No good trying Kings, they've filled their quota.' One picked up little hints of the way markets were drifting: got a feeling that it would perhaps be better to hold off selling for a space, or perhaps to sell quickly. I enjoyed those afternoons and the give and take of trading. I was told more than once that I drove a hard bargain but I expect most farmers were told that. Yet there were those who simply traded with one merchant and always accepted unquestioned the prices offered.

When it came to buying seed there was little room for manoeuvre. Only if you were buying large quantities or the merchant believed a low-price sprat could catch a mackerel in the shape of an order for other seed as well would he drop his price a bit.

Although barley was a free market, wheat was government controlled. The merchants didn't like it; on the whole farmers complained but did. Both parties got a fair price – but the merchants stood no risk of not finding a market, money for old rope.

Oats were consumed at home. The horses and cattle between them ate all we grew – well nearly all. Twice only and with a feeling of shame I sold a few tons to a racing stable, the shame eased by the very high price I screwed out of the owner. Beans were eaten on the farm. Horses got a few, but most went into the home-ground pig meal and cattle feed. On a few occasions I sold small lots of tic beans – these were smaller than the ordinary horse beans and often sold for tame pigeon food.

There was a terrific market for anything which could be described as bird seed. I don't like admitting it, but we actually made more money out of the weed seed threshed from one small field of barley than for the grain. Which cage-birds ate this rubbish beats me. It was the most awful stuff, the largest part being charlock seed and dust! There was very little grown during the war that couldn't find a buyer somewhere. I exclude from that the then-growing menace of wild oats, *Avena fatua*. Nothing I ever heard of would eat those hairy seeds which fell to the ground before the cereals they grew among were ripe. The worst thing about wild oats is that in the first year only half the seed germinates, leaving the other half for the following year. More cunning still, in the next year too only half the seeds germinate and so on and so on. This was a sequence which would have ensured their survival to eternity in cereal crops had it not been for the chemical controls introduced in the 1950s. But until then we hoed and pulled them in the sad knowledge they'd be back again next year. (They have not yet totally disappeared.)

Although my first love had been pigs, when I came to Appleacre and found room to rear substantial numbers of bullocks, I switched my allegiance. I liked to buy a number all the same age or weight – in bunches of twenty or thirty at a time. Some I got in open market, but it was difficult to get a really evenly matched lot of more than half a dozen, so I tended to

168

use one dealer from Essex who collected from markets and direct from farmers so many cattle that he could create more or less uniform bunches. And most important, he only bought and sold good-quality animals. So although he wasn't cheap, he was very reliable. For that trade he was a bit of an oddity. Cattle dealers used to dress in much the same clothes as the drovers – dirty brown slop coats and dark muck-stained trousers. Mr Mac stood out. He wore good tweeds, a brown trilby – the sort favoured by the fashion-conformist race-horse trainers – and clean brown boots. At market the other dealers addressed him as 'Mr Mac, sir' and the auctioneer clearly gave him the respect due to a valued client. Mac had a big area of grazing on the slopes of the Stour valley – three or four fields which could hold several hundred cattle. I'd give him a ring. 'Mac, I'm looking for a score or so of six-month steers. Have you got anything?' 'Might have, got a lot of good black and whites but you don't fancy them, I know. Still, now look I'm likely to have a bunch of Herefords up from the west next week. Come over and have a look, they are from the right place and – but you can make your mind up when you see them.' That sounded straightforward; he hadn't suitable cattle at that moment, but he would have, and I could see them in a week or so. The truth – as I discovered by accident – was rather different. A few days later on my way to a farm sale I passed by Mac's grazing land and noticed a considerable number of young Hereford steers grazing on the hillside. They were about the age and weight I was looking for.

Two days later I telephoned Mac and told him I'd seen some animals in his area I liked the look of and if they were his and if the price were right I'd be interested. He said they might be his and suggested I have a look at them. They were just what I wanted. We did a deal. We went back to his house to finalize transport arrangements and I remarked that he must have got the animals up from the West Country pretty fast. He gave me an old-fashioned look because he realized that I knew those cattle were not straight from a long journey packed tight in cattle trucks. Had they been, they would be bedraggled, mucky and ill at ease. Mac admitted he had already got them on his land when I first telephoned. 'But you know as well as I do, Guv'nor, that it's the lick of paint that sells the house, and a smart clean animal will outsell a rough one – that's why I keep them here for a week to settle before I try to sell. Of course you spotted them . . . a good eye . . .' Flattery never comes amiss. In all I got thirty-eight that day and filled the yards with about forty more within a month.

Although for some years Mac sold me more cattle than anyone else, I still went to market at least once a month, and if there was room at home I bought when I saw anything that looked good value. Sometimes I came unstuck.

At Ipswich market one Tuesday I was idly watching the cattle ring when a single white-faced steer came in, a very well-formed animal which was about the same size as some I had in a small yard behind the Dutch barn. It was a dull market and the auctioneer had difficulty in getting a first bid at all. I looked at it carefully: it seemed all right, except perhaps that its head seemed to belong to an older beast. Someone bid five pounds . . . ridiculous. It was surely worth twelve or even fourteen, so I nodded and in the end paid eight pounds for it and reckoned I'd got a good bargain.

Instead of putting it directly in the yard we unloaded it into a shed on its own for no other reason than I could get old Bob to give it a bit of extra feed for a day or two. I don't exactly know if it needed extra feed, but as old Bob said, 'That wholly wind it on in. That eat all the meal I give it, then that eat the clean straw as I littered down with. Never seen sich a hog for grub.' It was true, even as we watched it was 'winding in' great mouthfuls of straw as if life depended on it. But at the same time from its other end came a steady flow of very liquid dung. It never stopped. Had it been a week-old calf I'd have tried the old remedy and thrust a couple of hen's eggs down its throat – shells and all – but this thing was too old for that. We tried feeding only hay; we tried putting more dried beet pulp in the concentrate mixture, hoping to dry the brute out. But nothing worked: whatever it ate came out as fast as it went in – only nastier. Finally I called in the vet. He stuck his nose over the half-door into the box, took a quick glance and laughing, said, 'I see you've bought a right one this time, Mr B. Would you say it was a bit loose?' No comment from me – the beast was giving an excellent demonstration of its digestive disorders, splattering two walls and the door in one go. 'So what do we do – or rather what do you propose to do?' I enquired.

'Ah well now, that's the question. There are a number of drugs we could try but I shouldn't bother. To tell you the truth, this isn't the first time I've seen this brute; it's the third time and if you do as I suggest and send it to a different market from where you got it, I might earn a fee from some other farmer for telling him it's a hopeless case. Get rid of it, master!' I took his advice and packed the beast off to Sudbury market where it fetched fifteen pounds, giving me a small profit and a slightly dented conscience.

The vet was a rare visitor, a big man, very strong but never unnecessarily rough. I called him out one day to deal with a bullock which was badly bloated. Bloat or hoven is a distressing condition of ruminants which happens when feed, usually green feed, ferments in the animal causing the production of gas in the rumen. As more and more gas is produced, the animal swells. The rumen grows larger and tighter and unless caught in time the pressure is transferred to heart and lungs and the beast dies in agony. This one we caught just in time. The right-hand side of the beast was already blown up higher than its backbone, but it was still standing.

The vet got out his trochar, an eight-foot-long flexible hollow tube, and while I held the animal's head he gently eased it down its throat deeper and deeper until satisfied he'd got to the right spot. Then he drew out the stopper which sealed the end of the tube and the gas whistled out with terrific power and frightful stink. The side of the animal went down like a pricked balloon. It was saved. The vet said, 'You know your own business best, but if I were you I'd get shot of this fellow. Once they blow they're very liable to do so again and maybe next time you won't spot it quickly enough and it'll finish up at the hunt kennels.' I followed his advice and sent it to market for some other farmer to discover its weakness.

I bought stores at about five hundredweight and fattened them to nine or ten, during which time they consumed a great deal of hay, straw, oats, barley and beans, and left behind them two magnificent muckhills, which, after all, was half the reason for keeping yarded bullocks.

Sometimes I sold cattle in the open market. It is a very strange thing, but several times when I thought it was time for a bunch to go, a dealer would turn up with an offer to buy. It happened once just like that. I'd not said anything to anyone about selling when William Jolly, a dealer from near Clare, drove into our yard and asked if I had any cattle to sell. Yes, I had, and if he'd like to step into the shed – it was the big square one – he could make us an offer. I opened the heavy gate and we walked in. There were thirty-six bullocks lying cudding in the deep straw which got to their feet as we entered. Now these were not by any means animals I was proud of. They were really the leftovers from other batches, uneven as to weight and rather promiscuously bred; none bad, but few more than moderately good. Jolly walked in among them, and as he did so the cattle milled around, keeping still only when he did.

After about five minutes he came to the gate where I was standing. 'Mixed lot you got here, sir. Not much of a trade for them – long way off of finished, ain't they?' Yes, I knew that, but would he make an offer? He walked back among the cattle again and then. 'Yes, I'll give you nine-hundred and fifty. Doubt I s'lose money on 'em . . . trade's dead – too much rubbish about.' His method was standard. Trade was rotten, and by inference these particular cattle were rotten, too. I laughed, 'Come off it, you'll have to do a lot better than that. Try again.' He countered this by asking what I wanted for them. Of course I had a fair idea of their market value, but knowing the way dealers minds' work I said,

173

'O, I don't know . . . sixteen hundred . . . no, say sixteen hundred and fifty. I'd say that's about the figure: sixteen hundred and fifty.' Jolly grunted. '*You* may say, but the market won't stand it. Tell you what,' and he glanced at the cattle again. 'I'll give you thirteen-fifty – a fair price.'

At this point I almost agreed, for I'd calculated on average the thirty-six were worth near forty pounds apiece, which added up to fourteen hundred and forty pounds. But no, I'd push him a bit. He walked about among the cattle, mentally matching like with like, and after a bit came back with another offer.

'See here, I'll give you thirty-eight ten each for the four roans, thirty-five for the white face with the broken horn, thirty-two each for the seven black and whites . . .' 'Here, hold on a bit,' I said, and pulled out a cigarette packet to dot the figures down. 'OK, go ahead.' He went on, 'The ten black and whites, say thirty-nine; the ten Angus crosses, forty; and them four in the far corner, say forty-eight.' According to my hurried calculations this all added up to fourteen hundred and fifteen pounds, twenty-five pounds short of what I wanted. So I said no, not enough.

Jolly walked in among the cattle again and came back with a further set of figures broken down into new categories – eight instead of six. He rattled the figures off while I got them down on the other side of the cigarette packet. This time, and I hoped my calculations were correct, the figure came to a few pounds more than the fourteen hundred pounds forty I would have settled for. Jolly looked on as I went over the figures again and said, 'I don't know what you want written them figures down for, that's a good offer. Too good;

174

reckon I'll lose on it . . . anyhow I 'ont go no higher.' I agreed. 'All right, that's less than I was looking for [lie] but you'll save me the transport – take 'em away tomorrow?' He agreed and we slapped hands on it. Then the question of payment. 'How do you want it – cash or cheque?' And he pulled out a roll of notes the size of a pillow from the poacher's pocket in his jacket. 'Cheque please,' I said. He looked a little surprised and I guessed why. Was it not customary for farm managers to 'shave' a trifle off such deals for their personal benefit?

He stuffed the notes back in his pocket and handed me his cheque book to fill in. I asked, 'That's fourteen fifty-seven – right?' He nodded. 'You done the calcalaten, didn't yer?' I wrote the sum down, put in our name, dated it and handed it to him to sign. Leaning over the bonnet of his car where we had concluded the deal, he took his pen and arranging the cheque book vertically in front of him he wrote his name top to bottom starting with the Y of Jolly and finishing with the W of William. In fact he could neither read nor write, but what sort of calculator was in his uneducated head? How did he divide those thirty-six cattle into so many different groups and at the end come up with very close totals? I believe he had only a rough idea of what the total was, but he knew to a few shillings what each beast would fetch when he sold them on. I reckon it was a process which he himself could not have described or explained. I wondered whether he always relied on the honesty of the people he bought from over the years to give him the right totals? It remains a puzzle. I had several more deals with Jolly before he died, drowned while under the influence, or so it was rumoured. Despite his lack of scholarship, I was told he left a hatful of cash. If true I think it was unusual. Dealers carried a lot of money about but not much stayed home. Old Jolly was honest as dealers go and I rather admired him.

I reckon most cattle dealers started life as drovers and began by buying an odd animal here and another there, making a little each time and acting still as their own drovers. The auctioneers got to know them because they were the kind of men who would always buy the single animal no one else wanted, besides making themselves useful around and in the ring; they earned favours which auctioneers could give them. When they'd got enough money saved they branched out, probably hiring some grazing which meant they didn't have to sell what they had bought on the day. From there it was a short step up in the world. They tried to farm. Unfortunately, although there must have been exceptions, their hands were unsuited to the plough and they went bust. (I'm talking here of things as they were over fifty years ago: they may not be the same today, but the desire to move up the social ladder is probably as strong as ever.)

No two livestock markets are quite alike. They all share the same smell of dung, straw and dust, the crashing of iron gates and drovers' shouts, but it's the auctioneers who seem to set the tone – stamp their characters on them. The Bury ones seemed the most hard-selling and business-like, while the Ipswich ones were more jokey and exchanged badinage with the men round the ring. 'Come on, Mr Williams, you know you want them, another five bob won't break you, nor ten I reckon!' And Mr Williams responded by upping his bid, perhaps only because he was in the public eye and it was expected of him. The ploy didn't work every time, but it quite often did.

Markets are dramatic, exciting. Noise and movement, challenging situations: Shall I buy? Will it sell? What'll it fetch? These unspoken questions communicate themselves around the ring. Nobody shows it, but tension grows as the bids go in until, as the hammer falls – 'Lot fifty two, Jack Smith' – it eases until the next lot comes into the ring and the drama begins to build up all over again. In East Anglia it is not done for a farmer to 'bid up' his own livestock, and it is best to avoid being seen doing so. If you are, someone's sure to shout to the auctioneer, 'Let the gentleman have them!', which is what may happen. The crowd guffaws and the unfortunate farmer has then bought his own cattle – or whatever it is – and unless he can do a private deal before the market closes he will have to take the animals home – and pay the auctioneer's commission. In the small markets of Devon and Somerset – where in later years I used to buy cattle – farmers openly bid up the price – even going into the ring and telling the auctioneer to try harder.

We had our valuations done every year by the same firm, who were also estate agents and auctioneers. The valuer arrived in the morning and we went straightaway to look at the cattle and pigs and, when we had any, turkeys, geese and poultry. His estimate of their value – market value – was shrewd. It should have been: he was selling livestock at least once a week throughout the year, and quite likely had sold us some of the animals he was looking at. That part of the work was easy. Next on the list took us into the barn to count the sacks of threshed grain and feedstuffs. Of course he didn't really count everything, the idea of climbing over combe sacks stacked three high would not amuse him. He had to take my word for how much and the quality of the stuff: but he looked at it.

The same really applied to unthreshed crops in stacks and hay, stover and so on. He had to make his estimates on the information I was able or willing to give him. To walk round and measure a stack of corn and accurately gauge its worth when threshed is not possible, but as year followed year and we went through the same exercise together, I got to within a reasonable approximation.

After the stacks, the muckhills. The valuer stepped out the lengths, breadths and heights and then jumped up on top and walking about, stamping his feet and sometimes thrusting his stick into the mass, tried to estimate the density and thus the weight of the whole. The rest of the time was spent in the office, and the real business of the day began.

Knowing that in the first year I was bound to show a loss I wanted it to be a fairly large one, so as we sat talking over the figures in his notebook, I did my best to talk them down, because the lower the valuation this time, the easier it would be to show good figures at the end of the year. So if he thought we had five hundred combes of wheat and barley in stacks, I disagreed and said I'd be lucky to see even four hundred. His professional competence was in question? Not really. I had already made it clear what I wanted the outcome to be and he went as far as his conscience would allow – although I do not think conscience features very prominently in valuers' virtues.

'Now about the muck. What have you been feeding?

Hay and straw . . . I can put a figure on them, but what else?' This is where I present him with the costs of such feed as had been bought in . . . so many tons of sugar beet pulp, flaked maize and linseed cake: both those last two were hard to come by and very expensive. I had bills for them. But the less simple business was to put a figure on the quantities and value of the home-grown feed: barley meal and bean meal. The purpose of all this calculating was based on the understanding that the quality of the feed eaten by the cattle would be reflected in the quality and real value in terms of plant nutrients in the muck they produced.

The residual value of muck – that is *after* it has been put on the land and grown a crop – is important when land changes hands and everything from growing crops to the cost of cultivations is valued. I came to the conclusion that the annual valuation as shown in the accounts is usually a work of inspired imagination, but so long as the methods used each time are the same it helps to show the way the business is moving.

Chapter Fifteen

Men and Boys

By 1944 the war had still a while to run and great fleets of bombers were stacked in their hundreds, droning and circling overhead before leaving to knock hell out of German cities. One day it seemed there were even more than usual and Ernie asked Horry, who was loading a tumbril with him, how many were up there. Horry pushed back his cap and turning his face to the sky, counted with a long pause between each word, 'One . . . two . . . three . . .', then an even longer pause, followed triumphantly like one who has solved the puzzle, 'A lot!' I liked Horry. There was something appealing about his small, crumpled face – in a way rather like an old lady's, brown and innocent. Indeed the word 'innocent' in its Suffolk usage, meaning simple-minded, was absolutely accurate.

Horry, like most of the men, was in the Home Guard and I hope he got a medal. I once asked him what he did when on duty and his reply reassured me that his military training had been taken seriously.

'Well, fust the sergeant give out the rifles and we give them a bit of a polish. Then we fall out on patrol. Some on us set up in the top of the mill, and sometimes we walk about looken for nuns – but we ain't never sin none yet.'

'But if you do see one, what shall you do, Horry?'

'We got t'shoot 'em! That's what we a got ter do!'

'Are you sure you've got that right? Nuns are usually pretty harmless, you know.'

'No, not these aren't: they give us a talk about them. Yes, tha's right, we have to shoot 'em!'

He said this with such gusto and certainty that I feared for the safety of our high church rector who wore what looked a bit like a long black skirt and with his tricorn hat might well be mistaken for a dreaded nun. Fortunately the matter was never put to the test, which was just as well, for Horry, though it is unlikely, might just have hit what he aimed at. I never learned in any detail what the men who were not on watch at the top of the windmill did during the long nights, but a small outhouse sort of room at the back of the pub made a comfortable haven. One thing I am certain of. Those men would have been as brave as any professionals had the need arisen. One is grateful it never did.

It was inevitable I liked some men more than others. The tractor driver – Bill Betts – was certainly a favourite. He spoke more easily than most and told me more about the days before I came onto the scene than the others did, describing how they had tried to get the better of the previous far-from-loved manager. The fact that they were sent home on wet days when outside work was impossible – and it had to be exceedingly wet before it was wet enough for that – rankled. The convention was for the men to mend sacks in the barn on wet days. But too many wet days and the sacks were all mended and the men were sent home. 'Howsomever,' said Bill, 'if you can't find sacks with holes in 'em, you can easy *make* some – an' that's

181

what we done until the old b . . . see what we was up
to!'

Bill was alone in volunteering that he knocked off a
rabbit whenever he could. I expect he did the same for
pheasants, but he kept quiet about it. We were walking
down the long drift – a green lane or cart track – when
he suddenly put his hand into his pocket, whipped out
a catapult and quick as lightning let fly into the grassy
bank. I didn't even see what he had aimed at until
rustling grass stems led my eye to a rabbit in the last
throes.

I exclaimed, 'I never saw a rabbit – how did you
know it was there?' 'Ah . . . I jis see his eye glissning.
Tha's one thing about a rabbit, more 'n a hare. They
always keeps their eye open. An old hare will half shet
his eye, an' pheasants seem to keep theirs shut tight.
That make it harder to see 'em and hit 'em in the right

spot.' He always carried his 'catty' and used heavy ball-bearings as ammunition. 'They fly more true than a stone do.'

The second horseman, Jack Murkin, tall, dark and hatchet-faced, was another man easy to be with. Very slow of speech, but well able to speak his mind. Ordinarily, the men would respond to a direct question with some sort of an answer, but scarcely ever volunteered even a remark about something as banal as the weather. Jack was different. So much so that when he said something to the effect that they appreciated the certainty of work and pay come wet, come dry, I was quite shocked that he should have spoken about his feelings, which was something no one had done before.

I was not given to too much introspection, but hearing what Jack said, I suddenly realized how different my relationships with the men at Home Farm were from those here. At Home Farm I was one with them and, to a certain extent, one of them. Now there was a barrier. Of course we got on well enough together, but I suppose they didn't look for more than to be told what they should do – and it was my job to tell them. That was what they were used to: and I was used to it too – part of the accepted order of things.

Old Bob was easy. He talked to the cattle and the pigs and was particularly chatty with Janet, the house cow. 'Stand still, me dear . . . keep your blasted tail outa my ear 'ole, can't ye. Damn the flies, now stand still, won't ye!' He gave a cheerful sort of commentary as he went round littering, feeding or mucking out. He talked to his animals more than he did to me.

I would have preferred Jack rather than Jim as head horseman, but Jim had that position before Jack came on to the farm so it would have been impossible to alter their places in the hierarchy. Head horseman, as the title suggests, is a man of some importance. There was no other head of anything on the farm. He was responsible for feeding not only his own pair but all the horses on the farm: responsible too for their health and well-being. He had to be in the stables at least an hour before the other horsemen to mix the oats and chaff for the morning feed, dole it into the mangers and start the grooming. A good head horseman would make sure that every horse leaving the stables at the start of day was properly curry-combed, brushed and shining. I remember how George, who was head horseman at Home Farm, sent one of the under horseman back into the stable because his horse had a splash of dried mud on one leg.

The discipline at Appleacre was not so tight. Jim was a good enough ploughman but he did not have the respect and thus the authority that George had at Home Farm. Even the Guv'nor asked his opinion. No other man on the farm was ever consulted about anything of importance whatever.

The men I have spoken of so far are bright in my memory, but the others are drably dressed in old coats and caps. I see them straggling out to the fields from the cart lodge where the foreman gave them their orders for the day, and then as if camouflaged they melt into the dull browns and greens of the field. But I forget the two young boys, Bobby and Jim. These were different from the rest and much younger, Bobby straight from school, and Jim I suppose fifteen years old or so. They were poor. Nobody on the farm had much money but those two had nothing. They came to work with their lunches consisting of bread and 'pullet'. The bread was self-evident, and you had to pull the slices apart to see if there was anything between them. Quite often there was nothing, or at best a scrape of margarine or lard and an onion to go with it. What we did to help them was not enough, not by a long chalk.

Wages were low. The average agricultural wage went from forty shillings and five pence in 1940–1 to sixty-seven and ten in 1944–5. The boys got a lot less, the head horseman five to ten shillings more. Without overtime the standard working week was about fifty hours. Nobody was going to get fat on that. In later years when I took an active part in the National Farmers Union affairs I always voted for the increase in wages asked for by the National Union of Agricultural Workers at the annual review. The NFU stolidly

185

opposed any rise, and if a shilling were asked for, they'd suggest sixpence and it was normal for the 'independent' member of the tribunal to split the difference. The meanness baffled me then and still does today. In that connection I'm glad to say we behaved better than most and always paid something over the odds.

Few if any farmers would have suffered from quite substantial wage increases. The awful thing was, however, that the outcome of the review was expected and accepted by almost everyone. Farm workers came at the bottom of the wages scale . . . it was as if carved in stone. Farmers were in a strong position: they were saving the country from hunger and for that reason were enjoying a measure of popularity which seems only to happen during wars. The farm workers had a good case too, for where would the farmers be without them? They might well have put up a stiffer fight for more money than they did. Perhaps the union was weak – that I do not know – but I am positive that the idea of any sort of 'industrial action' never entered the minds of the workers in Suffolk during the war. It would be unpatriotic to take advantage of the situation. They were almost certainly unaware of how other workers were reaping larger rewards. How could they know? Two of our men took a daily paper – the *East Anglian Daily Times* – which was dedicated to supporting the farmers' position, and I think only three men had wireless sets. They were unknowing and isolated from any knowledge of national wage movements.

My own salary was not exactly munificent: £25 a month. But with the perks – house, car (business only), firewood and, of course, milk, butter and cheese – we lived well, and as benevolent old relatives died off we had no great financial worries. A very pleasant state of affairs although that would never stop me from worrying: nothing could!

John B had put me in an unfortunate position in regard to salary. He asked, 'What do you want?' And of course I put a low figure on it as I continued to do for the next fifteen years. Indeed I was grossly underpaid: all my own fault, and it didn't matter to me then, nor in retrospect does it now. I had freedom of action on the farm and treated it exactly as if I owned the place, which is exactly how I felt about it. John B never interfered.

I remember seeing only one woman working in the fields and that was at harvest during the time while we were still using the self-binders. She was old Bob's wife, Mrs Missen. As soon as the corn had been carted from the fields nearest her cottage, she was out gleaning. Day after day she walked up and down, bent double, picking up any straw with an ear on it and every loose ear from the ground, stuffing them into a combe sack as she went. It says something about the relationship between farmers and workers in that part of Suffolk that she first asked permission to glean. *Permission to glean!* I could scarcely believe my ears. At Home Farm the right to glean was taken for granted, although very few exercised it. It was a dying practice.

In earlier times before the self-binder was in common use and when corn was cut with a scythe, it was accepted that gleaning only started when the fields had been horse-raked. Now, except where a crop was badly lodged, the binder left little loose behind it – everything was bound into the sheaves. There was never enough left to warrant raking.

For day on day, directly the dew had dried off, old

Mrs Missen was out there going slowly up and down the fields dragging her sack behind her, a small, lonely figure dark against the bright stubble. Why did she do it? Why spend backbreaking hours under a hot sun for so little corn, perhaps no more than five stone? When I asked him, old Bob said, 'She want that fer har hins an' she allus fat a cockerel: one year she done a goose!' I am sure that is how she used the corn – for eggs and a fat bird, but the labour hardly balanced with the resulting products and I have a feeling she was unquestioningly doing what her mother, grandmother and many further generations back had done. They gleaned because they depended on it for their bread. They knew hunger. Her actions were instinctive.

At different times from 1943 to 1945 we had not only our two resident German POWs but gangs of them. This was after Henry and August had been repatriated. A large gang – twenty or thirty men in the charge of a Feldwebel or some such under-officer – came to help with sugar beet lifting. They arrived in a lorry and, stopping in the farmyard, jumped out, lined up more or less at attention ready to march off as soon as the order was given. They worked. It didn't matter what the weather was like, hail, rain, snow, they worked on non-stop; and in wet weather beet lifting, knocking and topping is beastly dirty cold work, hard on the hands and backs – the sort of job nobody in their right mind would ever want. The beet were lifted or loosened from the soil by horse or tractor lifter, one row at a time. Then the men, grasping a beet in each hand, knocked them together at arms' length to remove the soil left clinging to the roots. That done, the beet were laid in rows ready for the next operation which was to slash the green tops from them

188

and then throw the roots into heaps ready for carting from the field.

The Germans were a dour lot. They worked silently and methodically and at the end of each day they lined up on the headland facing the rows they had done and the Feldwebel walked along in front of the men looking at the rows of heaps. If so much as a single beet was out of line, the soldier responsible had to run and kick it into place. '*Alles in ordnung!*' Then they went back to camp.

What was noticeable was that although they were defeated, prisoners and acting farm labourers, often getting cold, wet and muddy, they never stopped being soldiers. Our men looked at them with great puzzlement.

Then, very near to if not just after the end of the war in Europe, we were invaded by Italian POWs. I managed to twist the arm of the WarAg, or the bit of it responsible for allocation of labour, and instead of the two or three we needed to help with harvest, we were sent ten or twelve.

From the moment their lorry rolled into the yard the farm was a different place. So much cheerful energy – a good deal of it misapplied – and so much song. I swear that I heard more operatic arias in the time they were with us than either before or since. And much sung so well. Never a silent moment, as when not singing they chattered non-stop. 'Like a lot of bloomin school gals wav'n their arms about, holleren and singen. They ain't like the Germans.' No, they certainly were not at all. Our men related to the dour Germans in a way they could not with the Italians, who seemed more foreign and alien in every way. They did not behave as sober working people should, neither did they win much

189

approval for their work. There were more of them than we needed and I think the foreman gave up trying to ensure they were all doing what they ought to have been.

Actually, and sensibly, about a third of them were always away out of sight in the woods and hedges. They were countrymen used to a much more primitive level of existence than our men and quick to take advantage of anything which would improve their lot. So while Antonio and Julio and Tommaso and one or two more were properly in place traving or on the corn stacks, Francesco, Giovanni, Andrea and Jesus were gathering ingredients for the midday meal. They snared rabbits, the occasional pheasant I expect, which with wild herbs – including wild garlic – went into the round-bellied iron stew pot hung Boy Scout fashion over an open fire. The Italians were astonished at the number of birds everywhere, and the haughty cock pheasants walking about within a stone's throw were completely baffling. Why was nobody shooting them? It was incomprehensible!

The great treat, better even than rabbit, was hedge-hog. One of the men – I think it was Giacomo – had a nose for the poor old hedgepigs and in the time the prisoners were with us he must have caught a dozen. They cooked them in the way the gypsies do, rolled in clay and baked in the glowing embers of the wood fire. When the clay was knocked off the hedgehog skin came with it and the meat was ready to be eaten. I am pretty sure the beast was killed first, but not eviscerated. Anyway, it was a delicacy. Our men were horrified, although passing by the cooking pot I heard Walter say, 'Blast, that wholly smell good. They 'ont come to no harm with a bellyful of that!' He was right: on top of whatever the army allowed them, their pot bubbling with wild meats, herbs, cabbage (they liked the kale tops), onions and potatoes gave them a healthy and nutritious diet, and they looked extremely well and happy on it. Again, very different from the Germans who looked grey and unhappy.

Giacomo and Jesus were a couple of clever lads. They found an area of osiers in a wet bit of Chipley Wood and made baskets with them. Heaven knows how many but Deirdre seemed to collect enough to last a lifetime – which one or two have! 'Are they strong?' asked Deirdre. 'Too shtronk, too shtronk, Signora!' Those two were the handiest and perhaps the craftiest ones. Jesus made really very good espadrilles from binder twine and Deirdre bought those too.

Jack said to me, 'I asked that little chap what his name was an' he writ it down for me. He put Jesus something or other. Is that right, d'ya think?' I said yes, that was his name. 'Quite common in Italy, and when you come to think about it we have Jacob and Peter and other names out of the Bible.' Jack looked puzzled. 'Yeah, tha's right, but Jesus, well . . . fer Chrisake!' And realizing he had fallen into a blasphemy trap, he laughed and said, 'I'll gootaheng!', a common expression of astonishment in Suffolk.

The Italians left after harvest and the farm was an infinitely less cheerful and quieter place thereafter. I missed the gaiety and the songs and chatter and so did the men. One wet day I walked into the barn where they were sitting in a circle mending sacks and their talk was all of how 'them Eyeties made their grub in that old iron pot and baskets and that'. Someone remarked he

191

didn't think they were all that clever, but Ernie said maybe not, but 'I doubt you couldn't make a basket as 'd hold anything: that's afore your time, ol' mate'. And that was true enough.

Sack mending was a relaxed occupation for the men, and the time was filled with story telling. Sitting on upturned bushel skeps or a half-filled bag of straw, they drew binder twine through the hard combe sacks, criss-crossing the twine so as to make a darn, or just cobbling two torn edges together. They talked chiefly about the crops and local affairs. Even after 'buzz bombs' had fallen less than a mile away, they remained a subject of conversation for only a short time. I had been up at the far end of the farm and watched one bomb as it cut out its engine and dived I thought close to where I was standing. I dropped flat and the bomb fell half a mile away, killing a Large Black sow and knocking the end of the farmhouse out. The only comment from the men was, 'Blast! I reckon you're lucky; good thing you bopped down do you might'a bin knocked down an' hut yrself.'

And that was that. I remember at the time thinking my story merited a bit more attention than that; dammit, I might have been killed!

On a few farms it was customary after harvest to have a feast for the men, or an outing. As I have said, the war had prevented travel to the coast, which had been wired and mined, and in Suffolk all the signposts had been taken away. Our first outing must have been as soon as the authorities allowed it. The men had never had one before and I thought they might like it. When I broached the matter, Horry piped up at once, 'Tha's a good idea. We was wonderin if ya'd do suthen like that. I wholly like a jollification!' Horry looked very pleased with this long speech but the expressions on the others' faces seemed to suggest he ought not have let fly that such a thing had been discussed. Anyway the idea went down well and I arranged for a bus big enough to take all the men and their wives to Clacton, which was their choice. In fact I don't recollect any other place even getting a mention. Some of them had been there before the war. I asked would they prefer a weekday or a Saturday: Saturday, unanimously.

You can't just go away from a farm with horses, cattle, pigs and so on to feed without leaving someone in charge. In this case there was no problem. The foreman volunteered to stay behind and look after everything. I tried to persuade him to go so that I could stay at home, but I rather think he didn't appreciate jollifications which could possibly involve the demon drink. I did not want to go either but when I told Jack I wouldn't be with them his reaction was swift – and surprising: 'No, that 'ont be right. We all reckon on you a'comen: everyone say so.' So that was that.

The bus, an elderly beaten–up relic from a local garage, went round the village picking up men and wives or the bachelors' girl friends. Horry was on his own but very smart in a brown suit and a cap three sizes too big for him. I had not seen any of the women before but they all looked tremendously respectable and dressed cheerfully in colourful frocks: much less formal than the men, who had something of an uncomfortable Sabbath about them. I could tell which men and women had been at school together: 'Hello, Daisy, how are ya then?' 'Half tidy Jim, mussen grumble.' And those who had not shared the school playground: 'Mornen, Missus Taylor, nice day f'r an outen.' 'That't is Bob, I doubt that 'ont rain today.' Although the men were not 'mister', the women were always given their married status.

There were some thirty aboard and we'd not been going for long before there was a bit of noise from the back as the first case of beer was opened. I knew enough of my responsibilities to have got two cases of beer, one of light and one of dark, as well as bottles of lemonade and ginger ale for the ladies on board. It had all vanished well before the bus finally drew up near the front in Clacton.

It was agreed that we'd all meet at the bus no later than five o'clock, but until then everyone would do as they pleased. It was too cold for swimming and anyway I'd brought no costume or towel, so I walked a mile or two along the shore and then back to the town and the pier where I failed to find 'What the Butler Saw' but caught a distant glimpse of a small bunch of the women. Apart from that in the seven hours we were there I never clapped eyes on anyone. I need not have worried whether the men had enjoyed themselves for it was quite obvious when all were finally assembled at the bus that they had been having a splendid time. They were laughing a lot. Jack was pushing Walter up the steps, 'Git you in bor . . . now put th'other foot up!' And young Bobby – probably the most sober – called out, 'Give a shove behind an watch out he don't kick!' The foreman's fears were amply justified. Drink had been taken.

Worse than that, the journey home was punctuated by stops for 'Just a quick one' at the Crown, the Bull, the White Horse and there may have been others of which I have no recollection. It was like this, the chaps absolutely insisted that I drink with them. This was a time when the differences acknowledged in the working day were put aside, forgotten, and 'Here's your good health. Drink up and have another.' Such good fellowship. If later I wondered if the camaraderie had something to do with the relative depths of our pockets, never mind. It was all . . . well to tell the truth, all too much. I remember being surprised, shocked even at some of the stories those hitherto decorous ladies were retailing, and was vaguely aware of two unsteady, wavering chaps leading an unsteady girl friend to her front door and having difficulty finding their way back to the bus.

Next morning old Bob came to the back door and asked what I had done with the milking pail. 'I looked everywhere. I found the milking stool a'floaten in the hoss pond, but I can't see the pail nowhere!' O dear. Yes, it must have been my fault. Apparently I had said I would milk the house cow when we got back from our outing to save old Bob, who was, as Jim said, 'Drunk and full to th'eyebrows: never sin him s'cheerful afore, never.'

So I had milked the cow and there was no problem about the pail for it stood empty just inside the back door. What was not right was the undergarment at the bottom of the pail through which in mistake for the proper muslin cloth I had strained the milk. 'I see the clorth on the line,' said Bob, and then spotting the knickers – for that's what the wretched thing was – he grabbed the pail and went off grinning to the cowshed.

The men heard all about it on the Monday, probably

well embroidered by old Bob, but I think it was a good thing, for they were much more relaxed with me thereafter. The Old Man, young though he was, was also human with human weaknesses.

Chapter Sixteen

The Local Scene

GOOD harvests, when the crops were decent and the dew (dag) was drawn off by the sun early in the morning and the days stayed dry, are the ones best to remember. We had good ones and some shockers. If I was there on the farm – and I tried to be during harvest – I used to walk out to the fields with Jim or the foreman to decide which was to be cut or carted. The older men used some of the same phrases I had learned at Home Farm. 'Ol' Phoebe'll be drawing the grease afore 'levenses' meant the sun will have us sweating before elevenses. Phoebe is Greek for the moon, Phoebus for the sun. I said as much to old Bob one day and he replied, 'Doubt you're right, us jus got it arse about face.' In Suffolk, to say, 'I doubt you are right' means 'I do not doubt you are right', and that certainly is a bit arse about!

We had strength to have one tractor and sometimes two horse-wagon teams carting at the same time – building two stacks simultaneously. Whenever possible I'd join with a horse team. It was good to be pitching or loading, to hear the shout 'Watcher gap' from the pitcher when the wagon was coming to a deep furrow and if not alerted the man on the wagon might lose balance and fall overboard. The pitchers – that is the men pitching the sheaves up to the loader – would call out 'Hold tight' when the last sheaf from a trave had gone up and the wagon would be moving forward. At that cry, an experienced horse would of its own accord move along far enough to bring the wagon opposite the next trave, but an uneducated horse might wait for the command 'Jis step' or be told 'Git on, Boxer' and have to be told when to stop.

Hard and hot work it certainly was, but during harvest there was a greater sense of camaraderie than at any other time in the farming year. For corn to be carried from the field and put up into stacks *demanded* everyone knowing what to do, how to do it and to 'cog' in together. At its best it was a smoothly operating business with a full wagon arriving at the stack as soon as the last one had been emptied, and once the operations had started no one had to be told what to do. With luck, at the end of the day it could be said, 'It's all sigarny' – a phrase considerably older than okay, which is what it means. It is derived from the name of Sir Garnet Wolsey, a young officer in the Crimea War who was a stickler for tidiness.

Bint was a word I heard less frequently in West than in East Suffolk. It is Arabic for girl, and you'd often hear a chap say, 'She's a pretty bint'. But to the soldiery, presumably those who served in the Sudan campaigns in the last century, it meant whore. So without trying, the word had returned to its original and pleasant meaning.

The red coats of long ago and the more recent khaki were worn out by the returning soldiers and their successors in the fields. By 1945 and the end of the war every other man seemed to be wearing a khaki overcoat either ex Home Guard or of more antique vintage. (In the '80s I still had a white naval duffle coat which I wore for pigeon shooting in snowy weather: Army and Navy Surplus Stores.)

Appleacre, as I have said, was an isolated place. The two nearest villages were Hundon over a mile away, and Stradishall, which was even further. Apart from salesmen and the few friends who could find enough petrol to reach us, we had no visitors I can remember, and the one and only caller was the parish priest, Father Weskitt. He was a remarkable man – the one whom I feared Horry could mistake for a nun – who regularly walked the long windy road between Hundon and Stradishall. His long cassock flapping round his legs, and tricorn hat on his head, he strode along reading a Greek Testament held about four inches from his nose, for his sight was grievously impaired. I had come into the house one afternoon to find him sitting in the school room where Deirdre was darning socks.

We had got as far as saying we were not churchgoers when our four-year-old son Roger came into the room. He took one look at this tall, sinister, black-clad figure and, alarmed, sidled round to take hold of his mother's skirt. Keeping a watchful eye on the vicar, and obviously wanting to remove himself as soon as possible, he asked, 'Where are my effing boots?' Deirdre and I were thrown into some confusion at this totally unexpected and never-before-heard language, but the vicar didn't seem at all embarrassed: perhaps he didn't even hear it. Anyway he turned up at intervals thereafter for a cup of tea and a bun. A widower, perhaps he just wanted a little company, although I would not have thought ours would be the first choice to look for it. I liked him, I liked the unselfconscious way he spoke of 'having breakfast alone in church with Jesus every morning', how he had seen Him more than once under the trees in the churchyard. He achieved fame in later years as being the oldest and longest ever incumbent of one Suffolk parish.

An earlier priest of the parish wrote a book concerned with the numerous witches who plagued the place. That was earlier this century, but they were still around, and all the crashes on Stradishall airfield during the war were laid at the door of an old woman whose cottage had been knocked down to make room for a runway. She laid a curse on the place, and lo! crashes there were! Another old woman living in the village was a witch: everyone knew her and was afraid of her. I tried joking about it but by the expression on old Bob's face in particular I knew it was no joking matter. She wasn't a white witch but a very black one, and not to get on the wrong side of. I think, although I knew nothing of this at the time, I may have been sensitive to something malevolent in the area, for I swore to Deirdre that one night making my way across the field at the back of the house I saw a tall, dark figure loping along on the top of the hedge. That was the year when smoke from huge forest fires in Canada rose into the upper atmosphere and drifted over Britain. The minute particles caused diffraction of light and turned the moon green. I do mean green and I had not been drinking. This phenomenon had a straightforward scientific foundation, but as for the witches. . . .

I reckon there were a few active relics of medieval belief still lingering in the southern parts of the Risbridge Hundred, and if they took tangible form from time to time it would not have surprised me. Even today, who in Suffolk would bring a bunch of the heavily scented whitethorn 'may' into the house lest it draws in a death with it? Every boy, when I was young, knew that if you killed a robin you would sooner or later break your leg. Even to take a robin's egg was hazardous, yet no other bird had such dangers attached to it.

Long before we left the farm we felt there was something about the house which from time to time caused unease. We were sitting one evening when suddenly the air became perfumed with a cosmetic sort of scent which was quite inexplicable. Equally the girl in a blue dress who in broad summer daylight went into the upstairs lavatory and never came out would be difficult for me to explain. There was never enough of anything to scare us, but neither did it make us unduly cheerful.

With seventy acres of woodland we had a lot of pheasants and the arable acreage, even on that heavy land, sustained around ten to twelve good strong coveys of partridges, both the grey English and the red-legged Frenchmen, whose morning and evening calls – 'Chukka-chukka-chukka' sounded from the stubbles and beet fields.

There being so much game about I felt we should have a shoot. I thought it was the right thing to do. I invited seven or eight men farming in the district. It was late October but the weather had been open and the trees were still in full leaf. On the chosen morning a thick fog came down. We walked from the yard across the meadow and took our places along the wood drive. In the distance I could hear the beaters begin their scramble through the quarter and we waited . . . and waited. The fog grew more and more dense and instead of a salvo of shots aimed at scores of pheasant, only two guns were fired. Total bag one rabbit and one pigeon which *walked* out in front of a gun. Where the pheasants went to I have no idea, but the beaters got lost and we called it a day.

The next two shoots were better and respectable bags brought home: thirty-odd brace of pheasants and nine of partridge. I asked the same people each time if only because they seemed to expect it, but on the fourth – and as it turned out, the last but one formal battue, John B (who hadn't the remotest interest in shooting) sent us an Essex farmer he wanted to do a favour for. It was late in the season, so when he enquired, 'Are you shooting everything?', I supposed him to mean were we shooting hen pheasants as well as cocks, for it is common that late to leave the hen birds to provide the slaughter in the following year. As it happened we had almost too many birds so I said yes, we were shooting everything.

What I did not mean was that 'everything' included foxes, and at the end of the first drive I found a group of serious-looking guns standing round the corpse of a large dog fox which the sportsman from Essex, poor innocent, had given both barrels. It just happened that the only man among the guns who hunted was the master of the local hunt. He was controlling himself with difficulty and turning an unnaturally dusky colour as he did so. Someone remarked, 'Comes from Essex . . . suppose he didn't know. Well, there it is. . . .' That was about all the excuse that could be found. Vulpicide in public was just not done, although what went on out of sight in the coverts of non-hunting farmers was quite another matter. Of course 'shooting farmers' destroyed foxes, but to publish the fact would mean social suicide in that part of West Suffolk.

It was important to choose shoot guests carefully so as to get the right mix. On our last formal shoot, I invited my old school history teacher, who was now farming about the same area of land as we were but just across the river Stour. As I introduced him I suddenly realized that he, and thereafter I, were damned. Max Morton was, I believe, the only Communist farmer in Britain. He didn't shout about it but his politics were well known and not appreciated. It was obvious from the look on the faces of his fellow guests that he was beyond the pale and positively the last person with whom any self-respecting farmer should associate, and their politeness extended to a distant nod. He was probably the only non-Conservative farmer they had ever even heard of.

It may not have been his politics so much as his practical socialism which made Max so unpopular in the farming fraternity. He went in for profit-sharing with his workers and in amounts which would in economic terms be hard to justify. He admitted that his system had disadvantages. No one ever left him and the population grew inexorably older. But he held to his principles through bad as well as good times, and when he finally sold the farm – that is when he was getting old and ill – every worker on the place got the cottage he was living in and a final hand-out of many thousand pounds. He was a gentle and most loveable man who was perhaps not quite so inclined to toe his party's line as was prudent. He once said to me, 'I'm afraid that if the comrades come to power, I shall be among the first to be shot!' So quite rightly he had doubts about the system.

At that time I was of two minds about foxhunting. On the one hand I felt it had earned a place in rural life if for no other reason than it had existed for so many centuries, and the sight of hounds streaming across the fields followed by the pink-coated riders thundering after them made a gallant scene. On the other hand, I put the men and women in the chase into the category of 'the unspeakable in pursuit of the uneatable'. It is an undeniable fact that once men or women are mounted they literally look down on everyone else; it is unavoidable. This, coupled with the fact that the majority of hunting people are well off and accustomed to being top dogs, adds to the superiority they commonly feel. I exaggerate a bit, for I have known a few men who have hunted all their lives and remain untainted by any sort of snobbery; but the general rule obtains.

The row was over cubbing. Appleacre Wood had an artificial earth. Two twelve-inch earthenware pipes in a ditch were set ten feet or so apart leading underground to a stout wooden box a foot below the surface of the wood and again about ten feet from the ditch. The idea was that the fox could approach this dry lair from the privacy of the ditch and nip through one of the pipes to the dry security of the box. Should it be threatened in any way, the beast would escape by the alternative pipe. These artificial earths – we had two, the other in Chipley Abbey Wood – were designed especially for the vixens to rear their cubs in comfort.

It was early one morning and hearing some commotion in the wood I walked over to find six or eight horsemen standing round among the trees by the entrances to the earth. The huntsman had put a terrier in but failed to bolt the fox, so now he was busy removing the grass and soil which disguised the site of the box. This done, he pulled open a lid on the top of the box and thrusting in a gloved arm drew out a wriggling cub. Holding it high for the hounds to see, he snapped one of its hind legs and just threw it to the hounds, which of course, killed it in seconds. I was both horrified and furious.

'What on earth do you think you are doing – what are you thinking of?' I asked the huntsman. 'Got to give hounds a taste before we start hunting proper,' he replied, whereupon a woman whom I took to be in charge of operations said, 'If young hounds aren't given a taste early in the season, they won't know what they are supposed to hunt.' Her tone jarred me. She spoke as if I had no right even to ask the question. Well, I had no horse except a high one, which I quickly mounted. 'Right. I shall not forget the cub's leg, nor shall I forget you. Now get the hell out of the wood, off the farm and understand that from now on you are altogether barred from this land.' And to add emphasis I waved my stick in what could have been interpreted as a threat!

Of course the real 'threat', which they understood but probably were not aware that I knew of, lay in the fact that hunting 'law' insists that a fox which has been dug out must be released and given ten minutes' grace before hounds are allowed to take up the chase. Let it be published that the huntsman had broken a fox's leg and thrown in into the jaws of his hounds and he, and the master, would have been in trouble. (That's the theory. In practice probably not.)

I was angry on several counts, not least being that the

hunt had never asked permission to chase over our land, which I count as shocking bad manners. That was nearly that, but a couple of years later a new MFH was appointed who rode over on his own and made a fulsome apology for past sins which he accompanied with a gift of two terrier pups. Weakly, perhaps, I gave in and said they could come back. Since it was well known that our woods were the only places where they could be certain of finding, he was suitably grateful and it was noticeable that on the few occasions the hunt came through the yard thereafter, caps were tipped and studied politeness prevailed.

Chapter Seventeen

Mechanization and Chemicals

A s the years went by I got some belated justice from the WarAg. First sign of a break was the arrival of Cambridge rolls. Next came the power-drive binder, an American machine, that was large and clumsy and made very untidy sheaves, but compared with our two old machines it whistled along, speeded the harvest and saved the horses.

In spring 1947 we took delivery of the revolutionary little grey Ferguson tractor. I could never sing its praises too highly. It ran on petrol, but was later adapted for TVO – tractor vaporizing oil – otherwise paraffin. The beauty of the machine was its system of three-point linkage by which implements were raised and lowered, putting them in or out of work at the touch of a finger. So here for the first time we had the fork lift and other

front-mounted implements as well as such things as circular saws, transport boxes and hoes – all could be moved from one place to another and put into and taken out of work without moving from the tractor seat. After years of the steady but slow job of horse-hoeing sugar beet, the Ferguson was simply marvellous. The acres we got over in a day – terrific! I think everyone fell in love with it and the competition among the men to use it was positively cutthroat. For the first time ever, here was a tool which more than matched the diversity of applications which had for centuries belonged to the horse.

If the Ferguson was an unqualified success, the next allocation was not. This was the longed-for combine harvester. When I told the foreman the news, he came pretty near to cheering. This was something we were of one mind about; a combine was desperately needed and now it was as near as could be – actually at Sale in Cheshire. It was on its way, but in its own time. We had almost finished harvest before the LNER notified us that it was awaiting collection from Clare Station, four miles away. We got it home behind the Fergy. Or rather we got that part which was on wheels home but had to send a trailer down for the numerous and heavy bits of the machine which we must attach to it. Essentially what we had was the body of the combine complete with engine in one piece and the rest in packing cases.

Cyril and I started to put the bits together. Unhappily for us there were no plans, no diagrams, no instructions. I telephoned the agents. 'Sorry Guv. We haven't got any ourselves but we are sending off to the States for some – you shall have 'em as soon as they come in.'

'And when will that be?' The reply wasn't exactly cheering. 'I couldn't say, Guv. No, I honestly couldn't say. Might be a week or a month, but we'll do our best . . . I'll ask the Boss to phone them. He tried once and never got through, but don't you worry, just as soon as possible you'll get the lot.'

I had to be reconciled to that and we started the battle to organize the bits and pieces into a coherent whole.

It took us a complete week. It was obvious where some pieces were intended to go but pure guesswork for others. As often as not the holes drilled for the bolts (all the mildest of mild steel with threads you'd swear were predisposed to stripping themselves) had been drilled just off centre, so we had to drill new ones. It was all a matter of trial and error, and as Cyril in an unusual burst of humour remarked as we got one bit in place at last, 'Five trials and four errors – we aren't exactly winning but we ain't lost yet!'

While we may not have been the best of mechanics, neither were the men who had conceived and created the monster. It was loathed and detested by everyone who ever had anything to do with it. This was something we had yet to learn, but as the last bolt was hammered into place, what we felt was triumph, modified slightly by the knowledge that there was about a hundredweight of left-over assorted nuts, bolts, washers, brackets and four lengths of curiously bent iron which looked as if they were designed specifically for something cunning but we never found out what.

We hitched the machine onto the Fordson and took it into a field of Harrisons Glory peas which had been cut and put into swathes with the toppler, a horse-drawn implement of great antiquity, or at least ours was. The combine had no pick-up reel so we raised the ordinary reel out of the way to leave the auger clear so that we could fork the peas by hand straight into it. It was not a job which called for much thought, so I put Horry and Fred at it. The tractor driver drew the combine forward to keep pace with the men as they walked slowly backwards forking in the peas as they went.

All went smoothly for about half an hour when all of a sudden the machine screamed and screeched, as if its bowels were being torn apart, and made the sort of crashing sounds that turn mechanics pale. It stopped dead. What had happened was that along with a forkful of peas, Horry had managed to pick up a flint the size of his own head (not an easy thing to do with a two-tine fork) and dropped it into the fast-spinning auger. We spent the rest of the day hammering out the badly twisted auger and found Horry another job. Apart from the auger, no lasting damage was done. The flint which must have been somewhat broken on first impact, travelled up the raddle and went into the concave where the drum shattered it into a million small pieces to join the peas in the sacks.

That combine had only two things to be said for it: one, the Meadows engine always started and ran perfectly, and two, the drum would thresh anything. I quite believe that if we had thrown coconuts in, it would have dealt with them. But that is the sum total of the machine's virtues. The rest was an engineer's and farmer's nightmare. It was a Minneapolis Moline. The name is deeply etched in my memory, and not only mine. The only two other owners of that abomination I ever knew almost broke down in tears when I mentioned the words Minneapolis Moline. They too had suffered. Working it was a punishment and if we managed to go for half an hour without the screens blocking or the hoists inside the trunking coming off their sprockets, or the reel throwing off its drive chain, we thought we were doing well. It was a three-man operation: a tractor driver, someone to take the sacks off as they filled, and another to raise and lower the cutter bar. That was the worst job because the operator stood in the full blast of dust being hurtled from the auger. No one wanted to work with it and although we used it as much as possible, it seemed to make no difference to the total time of harvest.

I occasionally dream of the ugly yellow monster, and another machine of the same colour: a yellow crawler tractor. I avoid naming it because I'm not absolutely certain who was responsible for its manufacture, nor even if it was American or British. Whichever and whoever, it was obviously put together by the last shift on a Friday when the conveyer belt was speeded up. Everything that could go wrong did so and to tell it in detail would be extremely tedious.

The first winter we had the brute was very wet. The last stretch of track from the far side of the farm into the yard became so churned up that the crawler had squishy liquid mud almost to the top of its tracks. Then overnight we had a tremendous frost and the mud froze every part of the tractor tracks solid. It took a day and a half before the driver could get it to move at all. That was no fault of the machine, but neither I, nor the foreman, nor the driver could be blamed for the gear-box failure, the steering clutches ditto and finally

211

such a combination of faults that I sold it at a loss.

I have since wondered how odd it was that these doubtful machines were trundled in my direction. Neither that particular combine nor the crawler were common – in fact I have met only two farmers who owned one or the other, and they too would rather forget about them. Perhaps the WarAg doing me less of a favour than I'd imagined? I reckon the USA had stuff they wanted to dump and the WarAg knew where to put it. I don't think I was paranoid.

We did get some good machinery. A Ransomes heavy baler designed to go behind the threshing drum used wires which had to be thrust through wooden blocks to separate one bale from the next. The two wires had to be twisted for each bale while the machine was in motion. Not a comfortable job: the wires were greased but always rusty. You had to wear gloves or suffer very sore hands.

Baling wire was used to mend fences, hang gates, join harness straps and chains. In fact you could say that during the depressed years and through the war, it was used so universally that it held farms together. The baler was also used in the field at haysel. Hay (or straw) was pushed to it on a wooden-tined sweep. The tractor sweep was a relatively new invention, and because it had no metal apart from the steel tips to the tines, it was free from WarAg control. The sweep, bought around 1945, was still in use ten years later, and the tines, two of them anyway, made of tremendously strong yet flexible pitch pine are still about the yard and seem indestructible.

The sweep was later superseded by the mobile twine-tying baler. Indeed the same could be said for almost every implement in the wartime farmyard. Most have been obsolete for many years. There are examples of most of them forgotten and rusting quietly away behind barns or pushed into yard corners concealed by brambles and nettles.

Hand hoeing was still necessary. Although we horse- and later tractor-hoed the root crops, we spent a huge amount of bent-backed labour over the hand hoe. The great weed enemy at that time was charlock, *Sinapis arvensis*, a rough-leaved, yellow-flowered pest which grew wherever the plough had been. It was a menace in roots because it germinated quickly and grew to smothering the young sugar beet and mangolds, or crops such as kale. It also flourished in cereal crops. Its leaves brought me out in a rash. It was enough to drive farmers mad and the men who hoed at it week after week hated it.

One afternoon John B brought me a sack of foul-smelling powder. It was an early pre-release of MCPA, the weedkiller which he said would probably kill charlock but would leave the cereals unharmed. We had a fifteen-acre field of barley which was being smothered in charlock and this was where I first used it. Having no machine to spread it, we used loosely woven sugar beet pulp bags, cut down so as to hold about twenty pounds of the powder. The men walked through the crop shaking the bags so the fine powder fell through the coarse mesh and onto the crop.

The following morning I went to look at the results. Amazing! The charlock, which only twelve hours earlier had stood erect and defiant, was now twisted, heads bent down and still visibly descending into death. 'Well, I'll gootaheng!' It was a marvel, and to see that the barley was, as promised, quite unaffected, was even better. The men were delighted, but they didn't much like handling the powder. There was a feeling that anything acting as ruthlessly as MCPA did might prove to have something nasty in store for the users as well as the charlock. So far as I know it didn't cause any serious ills although I got a rash from handling it – but so I did from the charlock.

MCPA was just the beginning of the great weed control revolution, the production of chemicals with selective properties which could distinguish between one plant and another. In the case of MCPA, it killed broad-leaved plants but not the cereals and grasses. Whatever we think about chemical control today, at the time it was a most welcome miracle. To think that we never need worry about charlock ever again, not in cereals anyway!

Wire netting, barbed wire, galvanized sheeting, iron pig troughs were just a few of the items which could only be got new by filling in forms and applying for permits to buy them. There were plenty more forms as well and they took up too much time and thought. Almost all animal feed not grown on the farm required permits. I had to apply for harvest rations – the special allocation of margarine, cheese, sugar and tea for men working the extra long hours during the corn harvest. These were very welcome and not ungenerous. Deirdre had the task of dividing up the goodies into fourteen exactly equal portions.

Chapter Eighteen

Family Life

HAVING one, two, three children in rapid succession gave us a family of five. The ordinary rations for that number made for easier catering than for two. Food went further, especially when one was registered as a vegetarian: extra cheese and the chance of buying luxuries such as dried bananas. Those came in boxes of fifty-six pounds, and lasted a long time.

We lived well and if I imagined I worked hard and earned it, I am sure Deirdre did. She was often darning socks by lamplight at eleven at night and then had to be up to make breakfast ready by seven-thirty. There was milk to skim, butter, cheese and pickles to make. Seventy pounds of marmalade a year, as well as bottled fruit — scores of Kilner jars stacked in the larder along with dried fruit and mushrooms. Add to this the business of keeping the children and their clothes clean — no washing machine, all done by hand.

We had some savage winters, one when the phone wires grew frost so thick they looked like ship's cables and broke under the weight of ice. The business of keeping pipes from freezing and of keeping us all warm was nearly a full time job and my efforts were not always successful. There was a small cooking range in the school room where we spent most of our indoor time, and feeding it with steam coal kept the room just about livable in. In the early days Deirdre often left the oven door open to help raise the temperature, and then had to shut it for a time before any attempt to bake. One day a small black kitten crept in it unnoticed. How long the creature had been in there before a faint scratching sound alerted us, I don't know, but when we opened the door out staggered a very hot, sad and thereafter educated kitten, whose whiskers instead of standing out straight, were beautifully curled. It suffered no other damage and lived on happily for many years after.

Home life was altogether happy. Minor worries like the time we found our eldest daughter sitting on the front doorsteps chewing a wine glass were, after a bit of a panic, got over without too much loss of blood, as was the time we discovered the same child with copiously bleeding hands and mouth sucking two safety-razor blades.

Almost as traumatic was the time when, minutes before his grandmother was about to arrive on a first visit, our first son managed to cut his hair and then find some herring guts to rub over his head. He looked and smelled dreadful! We learned that small children are born mountaineers determined to reach whatever heights hold such wonders as matches, new-laid eggs and a list of other things which in due course we put on ever-higher shelves hopefully invisible to infant eyes.

I did some daft things. I put the four-year-old son in the Willys Jeep in bottom gear and let him drive it round the meadow. I didn't imagine he could make it go faster than I could walk or run, but he did, and it was just good luck that he drove in a circle and I was able to hop aboard and thus avoid having to explain my folly to a coroner. Two years later and he was happily rolling fields with the Fergy. Of course I was recklessly stupid to allow, let alone encourage, a boy of that age to do anything so potentially dangerous, but he was sensible and no harm came of it, nor of several other farm jobs which he enjoyed doing which are now barred from lads until they are fourteen.

During the six years on that farm we never had a 'go-away' holiday. Days off, rare enough, were enjoyed with friends either on the farm or near at hand. The coast was closed during the war and dangerous for a long time after because of buried land mines and the rusting spikes of coastal defences just below low tide level. So being of a generation born during one depression and living through the thirties until the war meant we virtually had no holidays at all. We missed the sea but could swim in the Stour when I had enough petrol to get the family there.

Deirdre visited her parents in the West Country, taking the infants with her by train. The two eldest sat with her while the most recent was bundled in a sort of papoose – a scarf sown up along the long edges and bottom, tightly fitting and leaving no room for the babe to fall out. She was put up on the luggage rack, causing some consternation when a lady tried to put a suitcase on top of her.

I was left to look after myself for a week, and while not admitting to enjoying the strangely silent house, I got by on a diet of home-made brown bread and butter, a large Suffolk sweet-cure ham (from one of our own pigs), mustard and pickles and half a dozen bottles of good Beaujolais. Other than a cup of tea or coffee I ate and drank nothing else and never felt better in my life.

Deirdre had added the garden to her schedule and where speargrass had flourished there was a semblance of a lawn. Flower beds flourished and home-grown fruit and vegetables tasted better than anything from the shops. To say that is not to say much: shopping was never a regular weekly feature, more a matter of chance when I had to go to market or to Clare for a gallon or two of plain petrol. To be found with red-dyed petrol in your car tank was a crime. On the one and only occasion when the garage stopped filling me up with the red stuff after a pint or so had gone in, I was 'dipped' in Bury . . . and it didn't show!

Chapter Nineteen

Good Days, Bad Days

BY autumn 1947 the farm was running smoothly. The yield from sugar beet, a crop I disliked, had gone up from around nine tons an acre in '43 to twelve. Laughably little by today's standards, but then not too bad; it paid to grow for the sugar, and the tops were a bonus, as was the dried pulp fed to the yarded bullocks. Winter sowing that year went well and prospects looked pretty good. I had mapped out plans for improvements designed to be carried out over the next five years: more Dutch barns, two more bullock yards and an extension to the piggery. I was pretty relaxed. I no longer had to spend so much time at Maidenhead, so I was now at home nearly full time and happy to be so.

The only concern was the weather. Today, power-harrows and cultivators convert the most unlikely soil conditions – whether puggy, sodden or dried like fired clay – to tilths fine enough for autumn or spring drilling. We were not so blessed. We had to rely on the right sequences of weather, of frost and thaw, wet and dry, wind and sun before drilling could start. There is nothing anyone can do to change the weather or speed or slow down the inexorable roll of the seasons. These are things you have to work with and it is knowing that whatever the weather in its season, you are doing the best that can be done at the time which brings confidence and contentment.

Of course I didn't always get it right. Once I got it all wrong. We had a very wet winter and I ploughed one particular field when it was wet as muck. Then in the spring we suffered an exceptionally hot dry spell. I sent Bill Betts out with the 10/20 International to cultivate it and went off to look at work elsewhere. After an hour or so I walked down the drive to see how Bill was doing. From a hundred yards off I could see all was not well. The tractor was veering from side to side, bucking up and down, rocking and rearing as it moved across the furrows like a ship in a heavy sea, so much so that Bill said he couldn't go on.

'Sorry, Gov'nor, that's no good. I can't hold it and my arms is damn near pulled off at the showder. I can tell you, turning at the top there I thought we was goen to tip right over!' Then he used an expression I have never heard outside Suffolk, 'The clods is big as hosses' heads,' which is an accurate description for a field so rough and hard that to walk over it was to risk a sprained ankle or worse.

To do anything with heavy clay that is baked hard right through calls for patience and rain, not a tractor and cultivator. Perhaps I remember that field in that particular year because it happened to be one of our three roadside fields and thus open to notice by every passer-by. I was not alone in wishing to show the best face rather than the worst to the farming population, who don't go about with their eyes shut. (My old Gov'nor at Home Farm could recite not only the sequence of crops over a decade and more of every roadside field for miles around, but which crops had been good, which had failed and why.)

The men's seeming contentment with the way the farm was running was far and away the most important factor making me feel easy. They were cheerful and if there were niggles sometimes about who did what – some jobs such as thatcher's mate were detested – there was never trouble over pay. We paid a bit over the odds – a few shillings above the miserable statutory minimum – and most piece-work, where payment is always a source of contention, was done by outsiders. The atmosphere was relaxed.

Horry made a joke. In fact he made several, but one is especially memorable. It was a Saturday morning and Cyril the foreman was handing out the wage packets to the line of men standing in the cart lodge. As usual Horry was last in line and getting to him Cyril said, 'Now Horry, I reckon you've had yours, haven't you?' But Horry wasn't having that. He held out his hand for the packet and with the grave air of a man repeating an age-old truth said, 'Ah no I ain't. You ain't give it me yet. You can't citch a young bird on old chaff!' The chaps burst into roars of laughter at this and Horry looked delighted. His tiny round face wrinkled into a wide smile which spread from ear to ear. It is wonderful to find yourself appreciated. I was never sure if Horry knew he was being funny or not. Comparing himself to a young bird was enough in itself, but the added touch of 'old chaff' is good round Suffolk humour. I admit, though, you have to know something about the art of catching sparrows to appreciate the full flavour of it.

Banana skin jokes were often not so funny. Old

Walter's boy was never allowed to forget the day when he put his hand into a rabbit burrow and drew it out, not with a rabbit, but his own favourite ferret firmly attached by its wicked fangs to his thumb. 'Gootaheng! I never hear no one holler like that afore. He shruck worse'n he were haven his throat cut!' On the whole though, I'm inclined to think that cold clay doesn't generate humour in the way that light land living does.

I'm sure I would not have been so relaxed and cheerful had the farm not been making money. It did not generate huge profits, but sufficient to justify the way I was managing it. John B was pretty easily satisfied on that score. I was concerned at the substantial loss we recorded for the first year and the just-broke-even accounts in the second, but he was always optimistic and when we made a decent surplus in the third he was as happy as I was.

In some ways we had it easy. The government inputs were mostly well placed and very large. The subsidies on ditching an draining and liming were enormously important at the time as was the availability of cheap POW and Displaced Persons labour. These meant that farmers everywhere were being helped to improve the basis for good productive farms which would last for decades.

Increased yields and profits perhaps boosted my ego more than it needed but there was another thing which helped. Early in the war the WarAg had surveyed every farm in the country and put them in category A, B or C, and Appleacre was graded C. In theory the WarAg officials, assisted (or guided more likely) by a panel of farmers generally acknowledged to be 'sound' men, were supposed to visit every B and C farm, report to the Ministry and advise the occupier as to what he should do to improve matters.

We had been in occupation for no more then a twelve-month when the panel arrived to make their first inspection and evaluation. I assume they were satisfied at what they saw – the draining in particular – because I was more closely questioned about the number of partridge coveys and pheasants on the place than anything else. Now why was that I wonder? I never asked and was never told what they reported to higher authority but two years later and without further inspection I was informed we were in Category A. John B said it should be alpha plus.

Memory is rarely quite as accurate as we think. We remember that childhood summer holidays were made up of long hot sunny days, with maybe just one wet day? Farmers find it a lot easier to recall disasters and the times when everything seemed to conspire against them. There are a good many I shall not forget, some serious and some just annoying.

We reared about a hundred turkeys every year. Now turkeys are the most stupid creatures on earth and I soon learned they had to be kept tightly under control in order to frustrate their desire to commit suicide by drowning in the horse pond or running off and getting eaten by foxes. After losing two or three – one drowned, two beheaded – we made a large wire netted pen with a shed open on one side where they could go at night or in bad weather. One summer evening at about nine o'clock we had a cracking storm. Lightning flashed, thunder rolled round and round with an occasional bang so loud it rattled window panes, while hail

223

and rain slashed down. It didn't last more than twenty minutes and as the rain eased and then stopped I went out to look for any damage which might have been done. Nothing that I could see had been struck but instead of going back indoors I thought to have a look at the turkeys. Those damn birds! I found them in a wet huddled heap in the corner of their shed. I went in and started to take the heap to pieces, pulling the birds from the top and chucking them to the other side of the shed. It was too late. At the bottom of the pile twenty-seven birds lay squashed, suffocated and decidedly dead. I knew what had happened. They stayed out during the early part of the evening when there was just a light rain, but when the lightning and thunder came on they rushed hysterically into the shed to bury their heads in one corner, climbing on top of each other, all trying to get furthest away from the storm and the noise. Even as I pulled the live ones out they tried frantically to get into another huddle. Daft things. The dead were too small to eat so they went on the muckhill. That was a lesson I ought not to have forgotten, but fifteen years later I lost a similar number from exactly the same cause – panicking, hysterical, stupid turkeys in a thunderstorm.

In that same year another storm cost us dear. It was in August and we had a fifteen-acre field of oats just ready to harvest when there was a terrific hailstorm, rightly called a tempest because it came on the back of a heavy wind. That hail threshed the oats as they stood. I would have expected the whole crop to lodge – to go down – but it didn't. The grain lay thick on the ground while the straw remained standing. Not one single grain was harvested. All the ploughing, cultivating, fertilizers and seed and ten months' work gone for nothing in a matter of minutes. I wished we had some kind of vacuum cleaner to pick up the oats.

Another disaster. A frightful screeching crash got me out of bed and into the yard where the wind was blowing a full gale. The noise was coming from the remains of the corrugated-iron roof of the Dutch barn, an antique home-made structure. Sheets of roof protesting loudly were being torn off and whirled away. Several sheets had already gone and were found almost a quarter of a mile away next day. My worry was not so much the barn as hay, straw and fertilizers inside it, especially the powdered fertilizer (no pelleted stuff yet) in hessian bags – not the waterproof plastic ones of today. Somehow, all in the dark, I managed to find a stack cloth, unroll it and drag it over as much as possible while sheets of iron flapped and rattled overhead, threatening at any moment to slice me up in a most unpleasant fashion. That storm cost us a bit as it did many more of the farmers whose land happened to be in the belt along which it swept.

Hardly a disaster, but I can easily remember the day when our eldest son, then aged four, managed to turn the tap on the tractor fuel tank and emptied it, flooding the yard. It stunk for weeks. Nor do I forget the second-hand power disc-harrow I bought which turned out to have a strictly non-functional and irreparable gear box. It stood under the elms at the top of the yard sneering at me, a weighty and immovable reminder of my folly.

There was plenty more evidence of errors I would rather forget. When an unobliging neighbour wouldn't lend me his long ladder, I went out and bought one, forty-five staves which would reach the house roof and

225

the tallest stack. Unfortunately when it was delivered I realized what I ought to have known. It was made of solid hardwood – oak probably – and weighed a ton. It took three men to raise the thing and even then it made hard work. Old Bob complained every time the ladder had to be moved, 'I reckon you had your eyes shet when you got this article, Gov'nor – and I doubt that 'ont last long neither.' He was right. While I was trying to mend the small section of Dutch barn roof worth saving after the wrecking tempest had done its worst, the ladder slipped off the end, fell and broke under its own weight. Not to waste it entirely I cut it in two and spliced and bound up the long fractures to make the two bits usable.

My brother once remarked that it is quite unnecessary to tell people of your errors and failures when you may be sure they will do it for you. So I will cease, although those who were aware of my shortcomings as a farmer on that farm at that time are now most likely confessing their own sins to the ultimate higher authority. If that is the case I trust one of them will repent growing a considerable acreage of bird seed in the middle of an innocent-looking field of wheat. Bird seed was fetching tremendously high prices. It was illegal to grow it, and worse, at a time when the country was short of food, downright immoral. Yet it was understandable. Those farmers who had gone through two great depressions when no one gave a damn for them were severely tempted to make up for those hard times and make the most of it while the going was good.

The farm presented much more complicated management problems than does the average farm of today. On a mixed farm the cattle, pigs and poultry all had to be looked at every day, and the changes in weather over the seasons meant reacting to the constantly changing land and crop conditions. Again, in order to get as close as possible to a traditional four- or five-course rotation we were growing a wide range of crops, as many as ten: wheat, barley, oats, white clover, red clover, trefoil, beans and peas, sugar beet and potatoes.

There were times when I lost sleep worrying how to get the large amounts of bullock and pig muck we made out of the yards and onto the muckhills, or from the muckhills onto the land. I can hardly believe it myself now, but we used to take the muck from the yards and make the hill by drawing the tumbril loads over it. The horses pulled up a slope at one side and down a slope at the other. The higher the hill, the longer the slopes had to be so in the end you had a bow-shaped elevation. The idea behind the 'drawn-over' muckhill was that the weight of the loaded tumbrils pressed the muck down firmly and made for even rotting. I doubt if many farmers were doing this at that time and even fewer would have, as their fathers might have done, turned the muckhills once or even twice in order to get a well-rotted end product. I can't say the horses or the horsemen liked the 'drawn-over' dunghill method. It was bloody hard work, and the added value didn't justify it.

An annual worry was getting the sugar beet off and the land ploughed in time for it to weather and be fit for making spring tilths. I associate sugar beet in wet winters with horses up to their bellies in glutinous mud as they pulled their loads along what passed for the farm roadway. It was horrible. It would have been sense on that farm to have stopped beet growing altogether, but wedded as I was to the idea of maintaining a rotation, the idea never entered my head. I had to have a certain acreage of roots and that was all there was to it – stupid.

When I was at home, I would walk across the fields at least once a day to see how the men were doing – particularly when they were working in a gang, it might be hoeing or ditching. These are times when the pace tends to be the pace of the slowest and a little encouragement is helpful. Once on a wet day when the men were sack mending in the barn, I overheard young Bert remark, 'You can say what you like, but he never creep up on ya, do he?' I would like to have known which of my shortcomings had stimulated that remark in my defence. I know how men hate the Boss who creeps round corners to surprise his men in the hope of finding fault.

So I would start by looking at work going on and then go across the fields with a purpose – it could be to look at a wet place where a drain might have 'blown' or an outlet pipe been blocked by rabbits scrabbling at the bank. Equally likely I had no specific objective as I trudged from one field to another, but information was being garnered all the time. Small details: the presence of an unusual weed, signs of rabbit damage, just simply the state of the land itself. I make a point of saying 'I walked', for nowadays the Landrover and its numerous alien competitors have seduced farmers into remaining seated in heated comfort as they traverse their acres. I am sorry for them. They miss the doubtful pleasure in a wet winter of carrying half a stone of mud on each boot, or at the other extreme the delightful sensation – a sort of thrilling nubbliness underfoot – of the 'crumb' which says yes, it'll be ready to drill in the morning. There is a lot to be learned through the soles of your boots.

The time I liked best was going into a recently sown field to find the corn sprouted and showing in fine green lines from headland to headland, straight and even and unblurred by weeds. First germinations always excite notice. I'd come back from my walk and tell Deirdre, 'Barley's up on Twenty Acres.' And Walter or Ernie – any of the men – should they happen to see it first would be bound to mention the fact, 'I see Twenty Acres have got a hustle on, that's up nice this morning – h'ant bin in a week, hev it!' It takes us all the same way: a commonplace observation of an everyday miracle, and wonderfully cheering every time. There's no need to look at emerging corn crops every day, but sugar beet was a different matter, for as soon as the first leaves show above ground, the horse or tractor hoe needs to get in. It was a matter of beating the weeds, in particular, charlock which was our worst problem in that crop.

Charlock has a habit of emerging as soon as or before the sugar beet does. It will smother it and the beet rows will disappear beneath it unless it is caught quickly. With a modest infestation the beet can be distinguished from the charlock, but if the weed is at all thick it is extremely difficult. Get down on your knees and the difference between beet and charlock is obvious; the former has a shiny leaf and the latter a rough hairy one. This fact often means that hoeing with the sun at such an angle that the beet leaves shone was all right, but with the sun at the wrong angle, beet and charlock merged into a monotonous green and the man steering the hoes would swear his job was impossible.

At Home Farm one of my early jobs had been to lead the horse hoe. It was in a field where charlock was winning. The man on the hoe kept calling to me to pull the horse, 'To ye . . . from ye . . . no, blast, to ye.' I couldn't see the rows any better than he could and he finally swore, 'Hold hard bor. I only see one beet in that row and I cut that bugger out! We shall ha' to wait for the sun.'

Until we got the Fergy with its linked hoe we always had one man leading the horse and another man steering – four rows at a time and a tedious job it was. Being so much faster, the Fergy got over the land at a rate which meant the charlock could be beaten before it swamped the crop.

With 'pre-emergent' sprays which kill weeds before they come up, and selective sprays after, the business of hoeing is almost a thing of the past. Certainly sprays plus monogerm seed have banished the gangs of hand hoers in the beet fields.

It seemed there was never a time when I was without compelling reason to walk to one part of the farm or another. When harvest got near I'd do the round of the cereals to determine which field would be ready for cutting. That was not a hard task. Usually it is obvious when the grain is ripe. But knowing exactly when it is best to cut, when a day or two might mature the grain just that little bit extra and make a better malting sample because of it, is a matter for fine judgement. And then, after deciding to wait, down comes the rain, and so much for being clever.

I think the most delicate judgement was wanted when it came to harvesting clover seed. There were no defoliant sprays and as our combine did not have a pick-up reel, the crop had to be cut with a mower. The only hope of cutting and turning the swathe was when the crop was moist, for directly you touch dead mature dry clover the pods open and the seed falls to the ground and is lost. It was a matter of going gently, softly, softly and hoping the weather wouldn't make a sudden change and wreck your well-laid plans. Growing red clover could be worrying and white clover harvest was always anxious, but when everything went according to plan the results were so profitable and the seed itself such lovely stuff to handle it was very worth while.

Chapter Twenty

Favourite Places

THE two woods – Appleacre and Chipley, seventy acres in all – were nothing special. They had been, but the First World War saw the worthwhile timber cut, leaving trees which were just now beginning to be respectable. Mostly oak and ash, very little elm, some field maple – a species more commonly found in hedgerows – and an undergrowth of hazel and below that a ground cover of dog's mercury. Just as I had done at Justices, winter or summer, I never lost a chance of going into the woods.

Part of my long-term plan was to improve them by cutting out the dead and diseased stuff and the worst of the 'stag-headed' oaks to let light in and encourage natural regeneration. There were enough small but strong oak saplings to warrant spending a bit, but in the event I got most of the clearing in the smaller wood done for nothing. A trio of young men, led by a hefty bronzed fellow who looked as if he had only recently taken off his horned Viking helmet, brought a caravan into the wood, lived there for six months and did the job for nothing – rather for the firewood, which was in great demand.

The woods were important to me. Arable management, cropping, the business side of the farm and the family all demanded thought, created anxieties and sometimes brought triumphs, but it was the woods which gave me the deepest pleasure and relaxation. Here I felt a completely different person from the everyday one of filling in forms, doing accounts, tramping the fields and busy, busy, busy.

I have never felt lonely in an English wood. In fact I prefer to be alone in one. There is something about trees, especially large mature ones, that I find friendly and comforting. The sheer weight and solidity of a good oak, for instance, gives a sensation of primeval stability and permanence, peaceful and safe. I will go so far as to say that to be in a wood of large healthy trees gives rise in me to the same sort of emotion that being in an ancient cathedral does.

In the woods I could be myself and yet at the same time lose myself. To describe the effect on me of being in woods calls for poetry which is way beyond my power to produce. To say they give shelter from sun, wind and lashing rain; to mark how, when the fields outside are fast thawing from long, hard frosts, the interior of the wood remains an ice cave, so still, so bone cold; or to describe how in spring the light filters down to the earth through new pale green leaves, and the heart grows suddenly young and mysteriously light . . . it is all beyond me.

It isn't only the sights but the smells too, especially in autumn when the leaves have fallen. Dried oak leaves have a smell distinct from elm, and of course the sweet chestnut is markedly different, and even pleasanter. The timber of the sawn trees varies a lot: ash and sycamore are sweetish whereas elm, particularly when the bark is stripped, smells exactly like kippers and ash has an acid, buttery sort of smell.

233

I remember incidents embroidered in memory on the arboreal backcloth. There was a small clearing no bigger than a couple of tennis courts in the middle of Chipley Wood where I often sat. A fallen branch from one of the overhanging oaks made me a seat where I could sit quietly – thinking or dreaming or I don't know. I was there one autumn afternoon. On the far edge of the clearing from where I sat, the woodmen had burnt a heap of topwood trash leaving an area of fire ash.

I knew that wood, and even coal ash, was alleged to attract foxes (in fact some keepers set traps in bonfires for that very reason), but I had not anticipated seeing a fox anywhere that day. I had not walked especially quietly to get to my seat so it was quite a shock to see out of the corner of my eye a fine dog fox poke his nose from between the hazel undergrowth and then trot to the ash. Careful to turn my head very slowly, I watched him sniff at the ash, dab a paw in it, sniff again and, I suppose not finding it of much interest, sit on his haunches and scratch his ear. I was only thirty feet away and we were face to face. Surely he must see me! For maybe five minutes he stayed scratching and nibbling at a hind foot. Perhaps it had a thorn in it. From time to time he stopped grooming and turning his head from side to side looked about him. Perhaps to him I looked like a tree stump. But tree stumps don't have eyes and there was instant recognition of danger when our eyes met. Had I not looked straight at him I expect he would have lingered longer, but as it was he leaped sideways and in an instant turned and was off through the nuttery in such a hurry I could hear him run, rustling through the dark green dog's mercury and away, I assume, to the east side of the wood where the brambles were dense, the cover thick and humans never went. After he had gone I caught a faint whiff of his pungent, unmistakable foxy smell.

Keep still for long enough and you realize how much life is moving about in a wood. I've spent ages watching groups – flocks almost – of long-tailed tits 'working' an oak for ten minutes, creeping up and round every branch and twig, searching for insects, then moving off to the next oak and repeating the performance. The jays and magpies were quickest to spot an intruder. Still and silent as I might sit, those sharp-eyed and ever-wary birds would fly into sight, spot me at once and with loud cries – the equivalent of 'Watch out, human about' – scream off into the distance. (There were few magpies and even fewer jays at that time and they were nothing like the menace to the small bird population they became in the '80s and '90s.)

I was always surprised how a rabbit could suddenly appear without me having seen it arrive. It is as if they materialize out of nothing, lie belly down and nibble at the short grass – sometimes stretching up to sample a seed head, when they would usually become aware of me, the enemy – and scoot off.

At the end of harvest in 1947 the stackyard in the lea of Appleacre Wood held a long double row of stacks – wheat, oats, barley and beans, stover, trefoil (always pronounced *treefoil*) and kale – numbering in all not far short of forty. Well built and well thatched, they extended so far that on a misty morning when from a distance only the roofs could be seen, it was as if a small town of large houses had been mysteriously planted there. Within a very few years stackyards would vanish and the wealth they represented go into silos, but for the time being they gave me increasing satisfaction as from year to year the number grew.

It's doubtful if old Bob admired the line of stacks as much as I did. He had to thatch them and even with shanghaied assistants it was a hard job and always a race against time. As I have mentioned, thatcher's mate is not a favoured job. Knees get wet from 'drawing' the straw from the bed thrown down and soaked by the thatcher, and hands are made raw by 'paddling' the straw into yelms and carrying them up the ladder. It is hard work especially if the thatcher is on piece-work. He will cry, 'Yelm, yelm, come on, we ain't got all day. Hurry up, do the rain'll be on us afore we're done,' and the assistant will swear under his breath and long for the day to end. I know, for I once acted as thatcher's mate at Home Farm.

The stacks and the area between them and the wood offered shelter from the wind and hard weather which attracted wild life to their protection. There would always be a jackdaw or two (not encouraged because unlike rooks they pulled straw from the thatch), moorhens, clouds of finches and sparrows and pheasants as well. One day while standing with my back to a bean stack, I saw a hen pheasant scratching around the base of a wheat stack suddenly pick up a mouse in its beak. It held it, struggling, until with a quick toss of its head swallowed it. To judge by the way it stretched its neck upwards and outwards the mouse's passage was not an easy one. I once saw a cockerel – a big fellow – do the same thing, but I've never seen such a thing since.

Another observation made from the same vantage point was that wood pigeons coming in to roost,

236

especially in winter, fly at an angle with head and neck up, similar to the nose-up attitude of aeroplanes as they make their final approach to landing. The reason is, I believe, that their crops are stuffed so full of clover, kale or acorns that the sheer weight makes it necessary to fly at that angle. In the morning, having digested the load, they fly out straight and level from their roost. In summer when they have long feeding hours they have less need to stuff their crops so full at bed time.

Next to the woods, I liked the bullock yards. A new lot of steers soon got used to Bob and were not greatly worried when they pushed past him to get at the meal he was pouring into the mangers from a sack over his shoulder. Although he swore at them – 'Git out, git out you grit lump . . . mind out now . . . move over, blast ye!' – he was gentle with all the stock. If he sometimes whacked one over the rump with his fork in exaspera-tion, it seemed to be taken kindly with no hard feelings afterwards.

Whenever we got a new lot of bullocks in I spent some time in the yards among them. They didn't know me, and fresh from recent experience of being whacked in the sale ring and more beating to get them into trains or lorries, they were uneasy and anxious about what this new man might do. They moved as far from me as possible, backs to the walls and facing me. I stood stationary in the middle of the yard talking quietly to myself, 'Not a bad bunch . . . wonder where you were born . . . I bet this doesn't smell like Devon, does it? . . . Doubt you've ever eaten sugar beet pulp, have you. . . .'

They could see what I looked like and that I sounded more reassuring than the drovers who'd got them here, but that was not enough. Animals, all animals, rely more on what they learn by smelling the objects of their curiosity than by any other of their senses. I remained still. They watched until one braver than the rest would take a few steps nearer to me, wait a minute and then take a few more steps until only a yard or so away. The rest of the group did the same. They got nearer, stretching their necks out as far as possible, sniffing and sniffing, taking it all in. If I moved they jumped away, but if I then stood still they would move closer again. The final test would be for one beast to take a tentative lick on my jacket or breeches, but this was usually only after several visits to the yard. After a week or so there would be half a dozen sniffing and licking with their rough tongues at my clothes, or if offered, a hand.

It was wonderfully pleasant to walk into a yard of bullocks newly fed and lying deep in clean straw and sense their contentment. The deep half-belch as they bring up the cud and chew with sideways jaw movement is reminiscent of team managers in their box at a football match.

Chapter Twenty-one

Moving On

IT was December 1948 and so far so good. John B had
sent a message to say he would be coming in the
evening and I spent most of the day going right round
the farm. Two fields of bean, the wheats – six of White
Victor, three of Squarehead's Master and two of Yeoman
– were tillered nicely, and the two fields of Grey Winter
oats were better than I thought they might be because
they had not gone in under ideal conditions. Where the
fields should have been green they were; the drains were
running, for there had been a fair bit of rain, and the fact
that they were running into clean ditches reflected the
efforts over the years we had been there.

The long and imposing double row of corn and
fodder stacks and the hay and straw stacks told the same
tale of labour rewarded. The cattle, seventy-eight sleek
steers, were fattening and looked like doing as well as a
batch I'd sent off a week earlier. Even the pigs, where
in the summer we had some erysipelas, were a pleasant
sight as they snouted in the clean straw old Bob had just
put down.

Had I given the matter conscious thought, I would
have said the domestic scene was also pleasing. Deirdre
was well, the three infants were thriving and we had
even discussed putting in a bottled-gas cooker to replace

the paraffin one which was on its last legs. Deirdre had already reclaimed most of the garden but she had ambitious plans for the next spring: more flower beds, more vegetable beds, shrubs and fruit trees to add to the single but superbly flavoured greengage. So, yes, all in all I could say the establishment was in good shape and ready for a prosperous future.

It was dark when John B drove into the yard. We went into the sitting room where there was a good fire, and having settled down with our first pot of tea – for he came close to Wedgwood Benn in his capacity for drinking tea – I began to tell him how we had had a good year and why. In fact I was crowing like a cock on his dunghill. John B interjected a remark now and then but for the most part kept silent, showing no emotion as I even-handedly spoke of the good things and the bad.

John B was well known for never, or almost never, showing emotion of any kind. I suppose if I told him we had trebled my profit forecast, or had made a loss so huge I could see nothing for it but giving up, he might have raised an eyebrow. So I was only mildly surprised that as I painted an emphatically bright and rosy picture, he gave no more than a nod now and again of what I took to be approval and a grunt or two whose meaning I couldn't guess at. I went on for about twenty minutes or so and finished on an upbeat, saying that given the availability of a bit more machinery, the outlook for next year, the year after and the year after that, world-without-end, was very good indeed. That done, I had nothing further to say and I waited for him to round off the business part of the evening so that we could talk of other interests.

It was then to my astonishment he said, 'We have sold the farm.'

My mind was in turmoil. I could feel my face going cold and angry, and as the facts began to sink in, I felt worried and anxious. The family and my responsibility for them – something which had not overburdened my mind until that moment – loomed very large indeed. Where would I find another job with the security and the satisfaction which I had thought to enjoy for many more years?

John B went on. 'I know this has been rather un-expected and short notice, but my parent company insisted that nothing be said until negotiations were completed. Well, that happened only two days ago and I'm sorry that it will have come as a bit of a shock.'

Pouring another cup of tea for himself, John B said, 'Yes, if you start looking around at once – well, after Christmas say, I'm sure you will find a suitable farm and we can start all over again.'

'What size farm are you thinking of?' I asked. 'How much money is there to buy whatever it is? Where-abouts in the country?' And I added, 'Is it to be heavy or light land?' Coming from a man noted for a rapid analysis of any situation facing him, for being positive and down to earth, his answers to my questions were to say the least imprecise.

With another cup of tea and the last cigarette from the first packet, he said, 'Most of the answers to your questions are up to you. Size of farm of itself is not important and although it won't help you much, I'll just say it should be neither too small nor too large. As to money, total costs obviously depend on several factors of which acreage is only one. What I hope you will look for is a farm worth what you have to pay. But I add one proviso. Whatever the farm or the price, it should be a property which can be improved. That is something of a high-wire balancing act – anticipating running costs and calculating what you can afford to spend on improvements. Now about area. You know East Anglia and Suffolk in particular, so I suggest you first look for something in Suffolk – but south Norfolk or north Essex would do. Yes, preferably Suffolk.'

I felt this briefing was too brief. It left me with such a wide choice, doors open in every direction, that I wanted and pressed for more detail. But John B was not to be pushed. I'd got all the information I was going to get for the time being, and when I attempted to get more he said, 'I'll say one more thing and I regard it as perhaps the most important factor which I hope will inform your choice and that is it must be a place where you and Deirdre feel you will want to live and farm. The two things don't always go together, but it's essential they do.'

The evening finished with a third large pot of tea and Deirdre cooking plates of egg and bacon at eleven o'clock. He drove off and we retired to bed, heads buzzing with visions of a future which appeared to be without boundaries.

From that December until mid June the following year I was in a state of hyper mental and physical activity. Day and night I constantly shifted and shuffled the fixed factors around. They were simply stated. We had to leave this place in September. I had to find a suitable farm to move to on or very near the same date, and from December to Michaelmas the farm here must be

242

cultivated, crops sown and harvested and at the same time we must maintain a diminishing head of livestock so that when the moment to move arrived only the deadstock would have to be transported.

Deirdre and I found it very difficult – impossible really – to decide just what would suit us best. It was easier to find common ground in what we did *not* want. Neither of us wanted to live in the particular corner of West Suffolk where we then were; that was about the one single certainty we wholeheartedly agreed upon.

I suppose we had common ideals in mind – we favoured wooded landscape, fertile, well-drained soils, on or close to a river, decent buildings and a house large enough for a growing family and not too far from a village school. I was sure such farms existed and equally sure I would not find one such for sale. The search began in the first week of 1949. From that date on I took a half-dozen local Suffolk and Norfolk papers plus the farming papers, searching hopefully. For one or two days every week I travelled to look over anything which might come near what I was looking for.

I can remember only a few of the scores of farms we looked at. One I favoured was four hundred acres which, with its chapel or church, smithy and half a dozen cottages, made up what felt like a private village tucked away off the Bury–Ipswich highway, but well into East Suffolk. The land was heavy clay, which was a snag, but anyway the idea was smacked down when Deirdre saw the house: 'Too big, too grand, and I bet it's full of dry rot and probably the roof leaks.'

Had the absolute necessity to find a farm quickly not pressed so hard I would have enjoyed the search more than I did. Interesting people, eccentric people: I reckon the number of odd farmers in East Anglia exceeded the number of odd parsons, and that is saying a great deal.

Generally speaking I could see there would be no problem finding improvable farms. The harsh thirties, when there was no money, followed by the war years when it was next to impossible to find materials for repairs meant that wherever I went I found sagging roofs with slipping tiles, broken gutters, walls where the plaster was failing to hold tight to the laths, and buildings gently bowing earthwards, waiting for the next gale to finish them off. They were crying aloud for injections of money and energy. One could only guess at the state of the land, but I suspect it was often much better than the houses and buildings might seem to indicate.

On my list of farms to view was one which, if the estate agent's particulars were accurate, looked hopeful: three hundred and sixty acres, medium loam (a term which often means whatever you like it to mean), house of the right size, adequate buildings and not far from Hadleigh. The owner was elderly but hale, bright-eyed and cheerful. He invited me into the house and poured us a glass of sherry each. Old-fashioned furniture, photographs of his parents on the walls, farming journals on the table, it all looked comfortable, untidy and, since he was a long-term widower, just what one would expect. We chatted a bit about the state of farming and I asked him about the house: five bedrooms, a bath with running water, sitting and dining rooms, dairy and one or two passages and glory holes, plus a good dry cellar. I didn't see any of these – just the dining room where we sat. For some reason it is traditional for men to keep clear of inspecting the interiors of farmhouses.

We finished our sherry and taking his stick from the front passage he led me out to the yard and buildings. There wasn't much to say about them and in any case no need for me to do so, for he kept up a running commentary.

'Put the stables up m'self – 1910. Good as new still. Hoss kicked that door in last month; see I put a new bottom to it. Good as new again.' He spoke in short sentences, always pointing to the excellence of whatever we were looking at.

'See the barn roof. Thatched and wired in '25 and good for as long as you and me will be. Never stint bricks, tiles, thatch nor feed. It don't pay to stint. Things go down fast. Pays to use the best and don't wait about for next week. Now you'll want to look at a field or two I suppose. Take you where you want to go. Nothen to hide, nothen to be ashamed of; open book. We'll start up here.'

He led me up a dry cart track which divided the farm in half. Fields two deep on either side were all in just about perfect order. No wet spots, clean ditches and the thorn hedges well layered, pleached and stockproof. We went on looking at the cereals, the beans and clovers, in fact all there was to see.

His commentary never stopped. 'Never sold a stone of oats since I come here, an' only once a stack of stover. Had too much one year. All fed on the place – same with beans, hay, beet tops – don't like beet but it pays. Hogs, bullocks and hosses eats all of it and the straw is stamped in. Plenty of muck, plenty of muck. Bit of basic slag on the wild white clover and some kainite for the roots . . . that's about the mark. Don't buy what you can make for yourself; common sense, don't you agree?'

Having done the farm we returned to the house. A handsome young woman, the housekeeper I assumed, brought in two beer bottles and glasses and I began to assemble my thoughts on how to attack the matter of price. I did not get very far, no further than saying I liked the farm and if we could agree on terms, I'd be happy.

For the first time since we had met he was for a moment silent. He looked up at the ceiling, out of the window, took a sip of beer and then rather slowly and carefully said, 'I'm not goin' to sell. No, nothen against you, nothen at all, but I decided. Made my mind up when we come down into the yard. I 'on't sell. Not to you nor anyone.'

I began to expostulate. I had driven a number of miles to view a farm advertised for sale . . . and wasted my time. I would have been more forceful and much more indignant had I not liked the man as well as the farm. There must be a reason for his precipitate decision. There was. 'You think what you like – mad, I daresay – but I don't know, I suddenly didn't want to leave the place. Honest with you, wondered why I thought of it in the first place. I put a lot in – you sh'd have seen it when I bought it. Worked, never stopped, enjoyed it to tell you the truth. No, I'm sorry you come and had all the trouble, but I'm final! Doubt I couldn't be content anywhere else.'

That was that. I was sorry but glad in a way for him. I'm sure it was walking round the farm with a stranger, seeing it through other eyes, that made him realize how

246

much he would be losing: he had sold it to himself!

Farmers were selling up for many different reasons at that time but two kinds stood out. There were the elderly men who had no one to follow them – and I've been amazed at how many farmers just didn't breed at all. And there were the smaller number who had bought farms because ownership saved them from the war and their wives from the restrictions of the ration book. They found that farming didn't pay, that farmhouses were draughty, damp and expensive to heat and that the nearest cinema was too far off for the petrol available.

Chapter Twenty-two

Street Farm

O N May 6 1949 we drove eastward to Great Glemham, a small village midway between Framlingham and Saxmundham where Street Farm was advertised for sale. We found the farmhouse in a shallow valley almost opposite the village school and within a few hundred yards of the chapel, church, Crown Inn and Parish Room.

From the road, what little of the house could be seen above the roadside hedge was pleasant enough. We crossed a narrow and decaying brick bridge over the 'winter gull' – a wide ditch holding a stream after rain and a torrent when it poured – and up the short drive, flanked by mature oaks and elms, to the house, yards and buildings.

We stood for a bit taking in what we could see. The house, lath and plaster covering the timber frame, was a faded pink. It looked very like hundreds, even thousands, of Suffolk farmhouses with its plaster fallen away in places to leave the studwork exposed. It faced full south looking outwards across a small garden, and between it and the road a half-acre paddock was contained by iron park railings. The front door (rarely used) was draped behind a great writhing tangle of wistaria which spread sideways and upwards half covering all the front windows. It was in flower just enough to make us wonder at first if a nearby bean field was in bloom (a wonderful scent with fine aphrodisiac effects).

The south side of the roof was clay tiled, small ones held by oak pegs and covered in grey, green and orange lichens. The north side was solid emerald moss and I could only guess what the tiles were like. On the whole the roof looked waterproof and the chimney sound but there was a hole in the gable end big enough to drive a pony and cart through.

We were peering up at this when the owner, Mr Borley, appeared from the back of the house. He was a short, stout, round-bodied man with a round red face illuminated by child-innocent bright blue eyes.

'I see you're noticed the hole up there,' he said.

'Well, yes, we did just happen to notice it,' I said jokingly. 'And there's a window missing downstairs here and a boarded-up one upstairs. Putting those right will not come cheap.'

Mr Borley turned his gaze from the house and looked me straight in the eye. 'Ah, that's no problem and I can tell you mending the hole in the gable, putting in the windows and one or two more little things won't cost a penny. Not a penny!' He spoke enthusiastically – almost with relish. 'That's all War Damage. *They* have to put it to rights. I got the papers. Work starts any day now. Finished by the end of the month for certain and not a penny to pay!'

Was it a bomb, Mr Borley?' I asked.

'Not one. More like a dozen I reckon. American bomber crashed just on take-off and went straight into the park wall. I don't doubt his lordship will get War Damage too.'

I was curious, thinking of West Suffolk's nobility. Did the lord live locally?

'He lives in the big house – can't see it from here. Earl of Cranbrook. Don't interfere a lot but . . .' He stopped as if he had bitten his tongue.

'But what, Mr Borley?' Wanting to know the worst, I pressed him to continue.

He thought for a moment and spoke with considerable feeling. 'It's like this. I reckon he shoots more of my pheasants than I ever get his.' This was something I could understand and make allowances for because I know if there is one thing more likely to create ill feeling between neighbours than bad fences, it is pheasants. The suspicion is that 'your' birds are being enticed away by the neighbour feeding corn (even raisins in pre-war days) in adjacent coverts.

Leaving Deirdre to look over the house, Mr Borley and I toured the farm. The buildings were in a very bad state. Only the barn had a sound roof and the rest – stables, cart lodges, loose boxes – were plain awful. We passed through these without comment, but nearest the house was a tall, long construction with a corrugated-iron roof which was peppered with small holes but looked pretty good. Pointing to the roof Mr Borley said, 'That iron roof come from the First War – took it off of an aeroplane shed. I guarantee you won't find corrugated as thick as that anywhere today. Wonderful stuff, last forever. That's been treated, you see.'

We walked through a door to the engine shed. Now here was a marvel! A huge oil engine which by means of numerous belts and pulleys drove the mill in the barn. It was not just the size of the engine which astonished me, but the complicated arrangement of cross belts from a smaller engine standing on a bench across a passage which was used to start the big one. The belts, even the long main-drive belt, were all made up of old leather harness belly girths joined together with 'crocodile' fasteners. To walk through that shed when the engines were going was to risk scalping or worse by the fierce sharp fasteners as they whizzed from pulley to pulley across the gangway. It looked as if Heath Robinson had set it up in a moment of particular inspiration. But it did work.

I discovered that Mr Borley and his brother had invented the first mechanical sugar beet harvester, making frame, cutting sprockets and plain bearings by hand. It led others to complete the development and the brothers made not a penny from it. We walked on. There was a shed with an open door and just inside what I thought at first was a gleaming polished Rolls-Royce Silver Ghost, that most noble of motor carriages. But no, it was just the shining radiator with its pretty winged figure serving the elderly tractor upon which it was mounted.

Through the yards and buildings to the land. First, two small meadows, together less than five acres, with a pond where a family of mallards ducked out of sight under the overhanging thorn and brambles, and then on to the arable land. I asked if the land was all heavy. 'Yes, good stiff loam: what the agent say is right. Good stiff loam and very productive. In good heart; plenty of muck.' We came to a field named Elm Row. One patch of soil was noticeably darker than the rest. I suggested the reason was a 'blown' drain. My guide would have none of that. 'No, no, not at all. There's a little pond just beyond the hedge in that corner and the wellum [conduit] into the ditch beyond is blocked. Told a man to clear it this morning. Yes, I'd say, yes, a dry, well-drained field, one of the best on the farm.' Prodding his stick into the soil, he spoke emphatically. I thought well, he ought to know, but I'd eat my hat if that corner wasn't wet and had been for a long time.

I have to say that although I liked him at that, our first, meeting and indeed never lost an affection for him, when it came to describing the farm he told enough white lies to ice a royal wedding cake. It is strange. I don't think he really expected to be believed. His words were a matter of form.

We walked along cart tracks and looked at every field. The largest was only sixteen acres: the smallest two, but whichever way I looked the pattern was broken by a long strip of scrubby woodland, copses, hedges and areas which could safely be described as waste – outworn osier beds and bramble patches and outgrown hedges.

The field names were all on the map: Square Field, Further Square Field, Pond Field (a heron rose from it as we passed), Friars, Further Friars, Horse Hill, School Field (next to the village school), Butchers Meadow, Long Field, Barn Field and Sweffling Barn Field. And there were other names I have forgotten.

The picture I formed was of an ill-drained, difficult to work, very heavy land farm with only the Sixteen Acre Field moderately light and not needing draining. The woods and copses served only to harbour game and rabbits, and I noticed the headlands and beyond of all the fields bordering the woodland were nibbled down by rabbits. I commented on the osier bed, hinting it must be on very wet land. 'Osier bed? Yes, that is an osier bed and one of the most valuable assets on the farm. There's a basket maker out Wickham Market way always looking for golden osiers.' And he added, 'Do you see how that run down to the little copse at the bottom there – marked Heater Piece on the map – and on to the oak wood – Sovereigns Grove? Well, the birds fly out of there and into the osiers here: good high birds too.' (Sovereigns Grove was part of his lordship's land!)

In many ways the farm offered a very poor future. I kept thinking it made no sense to take on a farm which had been so ill farmed for so long, whose buildings were neither useful nor ornamental and so on and so on. But the place had a subtle appeal which I couldn't shake off. It suggested I ignore the wet fields, the weeds, the rabbits, the drains, buildings and *go for it!* Make something of it and enjoy doing it and living there. Still, the decision was not mine alone. Deirdre and ultimately John B had to be in favour too.

Deirdre had been all over the house. Briefly, two large bedrooms with low windows looking out over the valley, and two smaller bedrooms. There was a bathroom with a bath but no water supply. Downstairs, a large kitchen whose brick floor was worn into eight-inch wide shallow grooves by generations of boots showing how people walked from one door to another, and from kitchen to dairy or to the brewing and washing coppers which stood either side of a range. A passage led to the sitting room – the window blocked by the wistaria. From it there was a door to a small sort of study, another door which led to the back stairs, and two more – one the front door, the other to the cellar. I went down the wooden steps . . . it was bone dry.

At the end of our tour we concluded that other than the bath, the house had been untouched for the best part of a century. The beams – and there were plenty – and studwork had had so many coats of whitewash that all the surfaces and edges had melded into gentle curves.

There was no electricity, no water, no indoor lavatory: nothing 'improved' or modern. In fact it was not vastly different from the time it was built in 1540 or thereabouts. Perhaps it was that, the atmosphere, which excited us both.

After a very short talk between us, I told Mr Borley that subject to approval by my boss we would buy.

It was several days before I managed to contact John B and arrange his visit. He finally phoned to say he would meet me at three o'clock one afternoon at Street Farm. I got there in good time, but at four o'clock he had not turned up, nor at half-past. I filled in the time talking to Mr Borley about the farm and had a look at the little red-brick school just across the road: two classrooms and a teacher's house all under the same roof. It had been rebuilt in 1870. Ducal arms decorated the front but the separate privies outside were less impressive and their buckets were emptied over the fence into holes dug in the farm's School Field. The teaching I was told was very good: 'Nobody leave there as can't read nor write. The head teacher is wholly strict but they don't go in for thrashing like in my Dad's time!' This was encouraging for I could see our infants starting there.

I telephoned John B's offices but drew blanks. No one knew where he was. I hung on fuming. It was just short of nine o'clock when he finally turned into the yard, dark enough to have the car lights on. He jumped out, said he was sorry if I had been waiting – a remark I let pass in heavy silence – and he proposed that we walk the farm at once.

'But for God's sake, John. It's too dark. You'll hardly be able to see a thing!' He ignored my protest. 'It's the only time I've got free for at least a month – off to the United States the day after tomorrow. Come on! Look, it's a clear sky, full moon yesterday and I reckon I can see all I need to.' And with that optimistic forecast we started off.

I wanted him to see the buildings round the yard and pointed to the corrugated roof on the neathouse as worthy of inspection. But he would have none of it. 'You've seen the buildings – told me in your letter what they were like – let's get to the fields.'

This, I thought, is a hell of a way to view a farm you are thinking of buying, but that's what we did. We stopped for a moment at field gateways – Horse Hill and Long Field – and in a while came to Sweffling Barn Field, where the remains of the barn showed stark in the moonlight. For some reason John B was particularly interested in this relic (which I was not). He lighted a match, and pushing nettles aside bent down to peer at the foot of a remaining chunk of wall. 'What are you looking for?' I was puzzled and completely so when he stood up and said, 'Well, I was wondering if it had a damp course.' A damp course in that roofless hovel! Several things came into my mind but I kept quiet saying no more than that a few of the timbers were perhaps worth keeping for repairs.

John B was right about the moon. In the clear sky it hung, round and full, its white light washing the colour from the young corn, making shadow under the hedges and woods deepest black. The pond by the osier bed was jet black too and mysterious until a moorhen, alarmed at our passing, swam to cover, leaving ripples which turned the water to silver when they caught the moonlight momentarily.

It was beautiful. There had been a nightingale or two during the whole walk, but as we got to the bottom end of Pond Field it seemed that every bit of wood, every copse and hedge from Birch Covert to the osier bed and the majestic Sovereigns Grove, held a choir of competing nightingales, whose song swelling, ebbing, then swelling again made the whole landscape achingly lovely. It was almost too much. We stood still, not talking, just drinking in the sound for a full five minutes. It was magic.

It was going on for eleven o'clock by the time we got back to the yard. I pressed him to give me his decision quickly, and before he left for the United States. He promised to do so saying, 'It's very romantic by moon-light . . . I suppose you have made up your mind anyway.' And with that he jumped in his car and drove off.

I was left hanging until two days later when a short hand-written note arrived in the post. 'Go ahead. Buy. Pay as little as possible. Will be back end of month. Good luck.'

It was a relief. The uncertainty gone, I could concen-trate on finishing operations at Appleacre and negotiat-ing the purchase and the move to Great Glemham. Deirdre was delighted, which, as John B had said, mat-tered a great deal.

The rest of the year at Appleacre must have been pretty good. The harvest left us with more stacks than ever before despite the acres combined. Not that we did actually combine much: the machine . . . but I have expressed myself on that subject enough already. The sugar beet were in the ground and, along with the undersown clovers, the muck hills were valued and to be paid for by the incomer.

My time was split three ways: Appleacre, Street Farm and Maidenhead. My visits to the latter were merely a matter of putting in an appearance, checking the books and generally making sure the plant was running as it should. Most of what I did could have been done by telephone, but there was no one working there who could use a phone suffciently well to get a message over or take instruction! (Going to Maidenhead was not expensive. My diary notes: 'Clare–L'pool St: thirteen shillings and two pence. Bus to Paddington: sixpence. Paddington to Maidenhead: five shillings and fourpence . . . Total nineteen shillings.)

The business of planning for a smooth exit from Appleacre and an easy entry to Street got me on edge: how to ensure that the cattle and pigs too were fit for sale well in advance of Michaelmas Day. I did not want to take any livestock other than the one hundred turkeys which were already promised, and the same number of capons (cockerels chemically caponized by implanting a pill under the skin of the necks). They made huge weights but carried an enormous amount of yellow fat which no one really wanted; still, they were ordered and the money was good. The few geese, the house cow and the horses – just a pair of them – must move on the day we had entry, otherwise there would be nobody to do the feeding and milk the cow.

A great deal depended on the willingness of Mr Borley to organize his leavetaking with our entry in view. For his part he had nothing to leave of his on the place after the day. Not easy, because he was having an auction of all the deadstock and buyers rarely managed to clear the sale field in one day. Actually it was weeks before the last of the lots went: 'roll of barbed wire', 'rolls of wire netting', '22 sheets galvanized corrugated iron' (rusty, and they never did get removed) and odd lots of sacks and bits of machinery. I think the Rolls-Royce-radiatored tractor must have been kept by Mr Borley for it didn't appear in the sale catalogue.

I went to Street as often as I could and walked the fields again and again, each time wondering not so much how right I had been, but how wrong. Under pressure Mr Borley dropped his price from sixty to fifty-four pounds an acre, which sounded right enough, except that so many of those acres were unproductive scrubby woodland worth perhaps ten pounds an acre. Not to him though, because these small, scattered woods and bramble patches gave the cover for his pheasants and the noble earl's birds into the bargain. It didn't worry him that they also gave cover for rabbits. Not at all! During hard and especially snowy weather, he used to throw a tumbril load of mangolds out especially for them! What's more, the oldest man on the farm told me, 'I done it many a time an' I can tell you, what I put out in th' arternoon was all gone b'mornen,' adding, 'Th'ole man is mad at shooten, rabbits, birds an' pigeons. I known him spend all mornen looken fra runner he coulden' find the day afore.' Rabbits, and pigeons, would indeed prove a persistent nuisance (no myxomatosis yet).

But planning was the bugbear. Easy enough to plan for one year, but of course it never is just one year.

What is planted in one year on a field determines to some extent what is grown in the next and following years, and getting the balance right between arable and grass, between root crops and seed, is a complicated business made worse by the intervention of unreliable weather, prices, subsidies and government edicts. It was something of a shock to me to realize that planning and running a farm of two hundred and ten acres (or thereabouts) would be much harder than seven hundred acres. I skittered about between extreme pessimism and qualified optimism, but the decision had been mine and if the place proved uneconomic, I'd made the decision to buy and would have to accept the blame for it. As some kind person remarked, 'Once you've put your hand to the plough you must lie on it'!

The best thing was Deirdre's enthusiasm. She was always there to give cheer when it was most needed. And it was never needed more than on the pouring wet day when we moved the furniture and all our stuff in two large pantechnicons from a large house to this much smaller one. A good many pieces – bookcases, chests and tables – got shoved into a nag's stable, and it was many months before we got it all into the house.

The move went smoothly; the house cow had been milked, the rest of the stock installed and fed and the farm work would start on the morrow – and although we couldn't know it then would continue for the next decade and more.

It did not take many months to learn that the farm was in a worse state than I had hoped. I knew before we started that it is all wrong to look at a farm in the spring or early summer when everything looks at its best. November's the time, when emotions are chilled by wet and cold. I found many fields needed draining and one of the 'driest' fields on the whole farm turned out to be among the wettest. As for the 'pure water supply', well, it wasn't. The well outside the back door was our only source of water. It got its supply from the cattle yard, and when it rained the well filled – with dark water full of bits of straw! It was so black that you couldn't see your feet in the bath! But the children didn't suffer from stomach ills, and in fact they were remarkably healthy. Eventually, not waiting for the long-promised main water, I put in a deep bore to give unlimited water as hard as we had had at Appleacre.

By far the worst problem was weeds. My heart sank to see the vigorous growth of speargrass (couch or twitch) growing out of the fallowed ploughland. And later as the wild oats (*Avena fatua*) grew high above the barley and 'tame' oats, I realized they were going to be a major problem. They had company. On the one field of light land, I found broomrape (*Orobanchaceae*), corn marigold (*Chrysanthemum segetum*) and shepherd's-needle (*Scandix pectenveneris*) – all weeds difficult to get rid of, especially the corn marigold.

We – Deirdre mainly – endured many more years of oil lamps before the mains electricity finally arrived. And that great hole in the gable end – the one which five months earlier was going to be repaired 'at no cost, any day now' – was left for us to do and collect the War Damage payment.

Over the years I did of course improve the farm, but it was hard going and I was far from satisfied at the speed with which fields and buildings were treated. As expected we lost money for two years, broke even for two and made small profits in the remainder, nothing to

260

boast about. I enjoyed growing different crops such as
strawberry runners in the years when the chosen variety
was wiped from the market by a virus and canary seed –
a lovely crop ruined because when harvested it was contaminated by mouse dirt and the merchants wouldn't
look at it. Opium poppies was another bad idea, but
sweetcorn and calabrese did us proud.

The end of our time at Street Farm was a sad one.
John B, seriously ill, retired, and his company, which
included the farm, was taken in hand by the parent
company. I was easy about the change for on the day it
was announced, the chairman wrote to say my job was
guaranteed for, but not necessarily beyond, five years.
Yes . . . and within six months they had sold the farm
and I was out of a job and a home. Waving the chairman's letter at him, I did get a reasonably golden

handshake. But within a very short time, the parent company went bust, taking with it more money of ours in an 'Employees Deposit Scheme' than we had paid for the farm. It took long years and battles before we retrieved even part of it. Since when my advice is 'Never trust big business.'

Our active farming ended at Street Farm, and as much by accident as had been the case with so much of my life, before very long I was working in Africa and later in southeast Asia. Deirdre and I always looked back on the Street Farm years as among the happiest. We worked hard, reared five good children (who did learn to read and write and do sums at the village school) and for the most part lived in harmony with our neighbours, so all in all, yes, the living was good.

Other Titles from Old Pond Publishing

In a Long Day   DAVID KINDRED & ROGER SMITH
Two hundred captioned photographs of farm work and village life in Suffolk 1925–33. Paperback.

Land Girls at the Old Rectory   IRENE GRIMWOOD
Light-hearted, boisterous memories of land girls in Suffolk 1942–46. Paperback.

Harvest from Sickle to Satellite   BRIAN BELL
Video history showing reapers, combine harvesters and harvesting.

Power of the Past   BRIAN BELL
Gyrotillers, farm tractors and crawlers, earth-movers and other machines at work. Video.

Steam at Strumpshaw   BRIAN BELL
A video introduction to steam-powered traction engines, ploughing engines and other machines.

Ferguson Tractors   STUART GIBBARD
The story of the little grey Fergie and other Ferguson tractors and equipment. 65-minute video.

Free complete catalogue:

Old Pond Publishing
104 Valley Road, Ipswich IP1 4PA, United Kingdom
Phone / fax + 44 (0) 1473 210176
Website: www.oldpond.com
Email: enquiries@oldpond.com

About the Author

Born in Colchester, Essex in 1917, Hugh Barrett left school at sixteen to become a farm pupil. Following this he stuck mainly to farming, and from 1953 he also worked as a journalist and broadcaster, mostly on agricultural topics for BBC home and overseas services.

He became a lecturer at the Institute of Adult Education in the University of Dar Es Salaam where he helped organize what was then the world's largest mass adult education project. He went on to work for various government and non-government agencies on projects promoting health and agriculture in five African countries, including Uganda during the time of Idi Amin. Hugh's last major posting was to Thailand where he initiated the 'group learning' method of education for rural dwellers.

Hugh's first book *Early to Rise*, describing his time as a farm pupil, was published in 1967; *A Good Living* is its sequel. The romantic early days of Hugh's marriage to Deirdre are portrayed in this book and they remained happily married until her death in 1997. Hugh has five children, twelve grandchildren and three great-grandchildren. He lives near Halesworth in Suffolk.